boobs

Caitlin Press Inc.
8100 Alderwood Road,
Halfmoon Bay, BC V0N 1Y1
www.caitlin-press.com

Edited by Ruth Daniell
Text and cover design by Vici Johnstone
Printed in Canada

Caitlin Press Inc. acknowledges financial support from the Government of Canada through the Canada Book Fund and the Canada Council for the Arts, and from the Province of British Columbia through the British Columbia Arts Council and the Book Publisher's Tax Credit.

**Canada Council
for the Arts** **Conseil des Arts
du Canada** BRITISH COLUMBIA
ARTS COUNCIL
We acknowledge the support of the Province of British Columbia through the British Columbia Arts Council

Library and Archives Canada Cataloguing in Publication
Boobs : women explore what it means to have breasts
/ edited by Ruth Daniell.

ISBN 978-1-987915-05-1 (paperback)

    1. Breast — Literary collections. I. Daniell, Ruth, 1987-, editor

PS8237.B74B65 2016   C810.8'03561   C2015-908655-8

boobs

WOMEN EXPLORE WHAT IT
MEANS TO HAVE BREASTS

EDITED BY

RUTH DANIELL

CAITLIN PRESS

for the readers of this book, those with and without boobs

Contents

INTRODUCTION

Ruth Daniell

> How can you be so interested in them?… No, but serious-
> ly. They're just breasts. Every second person in the world
> has them… But they're odd looking. They're for milk. Your
> mother has them. You've seen a thousand of them. What's
> all the fuss about? — *Notting Hill* (1999)

Julia Roberts's character in *Notting Hill*, Anna Scott, is incredulous
about all the fuss that people make about breasts. After topless
photos of her are published without her consent she is rightly upset about all the negative attention this attracts to her. The uglier
aspects of that violation aside, she points out that it's a bit strange
that breasts are made out to be so exciting in the first place. After
all, they're not uncommon. And while it's abstractly bizarre to
consider — as Anna does — society's fixation on breasts it's not
hard to understand why those of us who actually have breasts
might fuss over them. Out of all the intimate body parts on female and male bodies, breasts are the most visible. Other body
parts are remarkable naked, but breasts are hard to miss even
when they're clothed. Sure, you can try to hide breasts in baggy
clothing, but they nevertheless remain much more conspicuous
than a vulva or a penis ever are. Out of all private parts, breasts
are incredibly public. Strangers can make observations about another's breasts in a way they can't about other body parts that
play important roles in how individuals form their identities. And
breasts do play important roles in how an individual forms their
identity, especially in relationship to their gender and sexuality
— and how others interpret their gender and sexuality. Breasts
are almost a form of communication: the outside world perceives
the owners of breasts in different ways depending on the size,
shape, colour of the breasts, depending on the ways that those
breasts are adorned, shown off, hidden. Those with breasts are

11

assumed to be modest or confident, naïve or experienced, smart or stupid, and any number of traits simply based on the visibility of their breasts. Breasts are celebrated or criticized as sexual objects. Breasts are similarly celebrated or criticized as sources of milk and the epitome of motherhood. They become symbols to the people who view them. But what does having breasts mean to the people who have them, want them, don't want them, or used to have them? How does having — or not having — breasts affect how we understand our identities as women? Simply put: what's all the fuss about?

Breasts — or the lack or loss of breasts — are often at the centre of the most defining experiences of women's lives: puberty, adolescence, aging, motherhood, sisterhood. Breasts play starring roles not just in glossy magazines and Hollywood movies but also in the everyday stories that so many of us face: stories about growing up, love, sex, friendship, jealousy, abuse, healing, and stories about department stores and the frustration of bra shopping. The following stories and poems are about breasts that cause pleasure and pain, embarrassment and pride, guilt and hope, sorrow and happiness, and comfort and fear. In this anthology, I have tried to compile as diverse a collection of these kinds of stories as I could — from writers of all ages, orientations, colours and backgrounds, including transgendered writers. Of course, it is impossible to reflect all forms of experience, so I do not claim that this anthology fulfills the task of representing everything that breasts could and do mean.

I want to acknowledge that this anthology includes a lot of pieces that specifically tackle the subject of breast cancer and breast cancer scares. When we first sent out the call for submissions, I expected to receive a diverse range of stories about breasts, and I knew and hoped that among the submissions I would receive stories about breast cancer, but I was surprised at the sheer number of stories about cancer that poured in. A quick search on the Canadian Breast Cancer Foundation website reminded me why this was the case: breast cancer is the most commonly diagnosed cancer in Canadian women, representing 26 percent of all newly diagnosed cancers in women (and 0.2 percentage of cancers in men). Although the survival rate for breast cancer has much improved since 1986, when breast cancer mortality was at its peak and the survival ratio was 79 percent (it's now 88 percent), it is estimated that 1 in 30 women in Canada die from breast cancer. According to the Foundation's statistics 25,000 Canadian women are diagnosed with breast cancer each year, including the year this book spent in production. This book is for those women, and for everyone whose lives have been changed by receiving or supporting a loved one with a breast cancer diagnosis. As the numbers suggest, that means this book is for everyone.

Dear reader, you have picked up this anthology for reasons only you know. I can't help but hope that among those reasons is that you love breasts — breasts in a general sense, but also the specific breasts of people you love. I hope you love your own breasts, if you have them. But if you have picked up this book, my experience tells me that you also probably don't like your breasts very much sometimes. Perhaps you think your boobs are too little. Perhaps you think your boobs are too big, or the wrong shape, or the nipples are weird, or they're just not as nice as your girlfriend's or your mother's. Perhaps your boobs have disappointed you in some way — they haven't given the sexual pleasure you wanted, or nursed your children how you hoped, or they cost you three hundred dollars in specialty bras each year. It's my hope that this book will remind you that you're not alone. Every second person in the world, and more besides, has had their breasts or lack of breasts (or lack of the kind of breasts they wanted) influence their sense of self. Breasts — no matter their shape or colour or size — are a big deal. Yes, they're just breasts. But they mean a lot more than that. Be kind to each other, and to yourself — and feel free to fuss.

Ruth Daniell

January 2016
Vancouver, BC

News Flash from the Fashion Magazines

Lorna Crozier

Breasts are back!
You can see them everywhere.
On movie screens, in restaurants,
at baseball games. You can feel them
bump against you in the subway
like friendly spaniels.
Big as melons they bob
behind grocery carts,
they pout under denim.
Breasts are back!
They won't stay locked up.
They shrink the space
in elevators, they leap
out of jogging bras,
find their own way
down the road, running
hand in hand. They wave
at you from buses,
swaying around corners
and swinging back. Oh,
how they move! Graceful
ballerinas, a *pas de deux*.
They rise and fall
under your grandmother's floral apron,
they flutter under your daughter's
T-shirt, small shy sparrows
learning to fly.
Breasts are back. On the beach
nipples peek from bikinis

as if they were eyes, wide open,
wanting to watch the sea.
Sailors rise from the Atlantic,
clutching their Mae Wests
for breasts are back.

But wait! Not just any breasts.
A breast should not be able to support
a pencil underneath it.
A breast must fit into a champagne glass,
not the beer mug you raise
to your mouth on a hot summer day.
A breast must have nipples
no bigger than a dime.
A breast must be hairless,
not even one or two small hairs
for your lover to remove
with his teeth. A breast must bear
no stretch marks, must be smooth
as alabaster, luminous as pearls.

Enough of that!
Let's stand up for breasts
any size, any colour,
breasts shaped like kiwi fruit,
like mandolins, like pouter pigeons,
breasts playful and shameless as puppies.
Breasts that pop buttons,
breasts with rose tattoos.
Let's give them the vote.
Let's make them mayor for the day.
Let's remember our old secret
loyalties, the first words
they placed in our mouths,
the sweet warm vowels

of our mother's milk
urging us toward our lives
before we even knew our names.
Breasts are back, let's shout it,
and they're here to stay!

Previously in *The Blue Hour of the Day: Selected Poems* (Toronto: McClelland & Stewart, 2007)

Variety Pack

Sara Graefe

"No woman is perfectly symmetrical," my mother reassured me, adjusting the straps on the training bra until they sat snug against my shoulders. We were crammed into a drab fitting room at our suburban Sears. I checked myself out in the full-length mirror, fighting back tears. I was fourteen, too old for my boobs to still be in training, but somehow my body had missed the memo. My left breast almost filled the small A-cup, but the right barely made an appearance. The bland beige fabric sagged sadly over the tiny bud. I knew my mom was trying her damnedest to make me feel better, but her placating words had precisely the opposite effect. Couldn't she see I was a freak? No one I knew had breasts as disproportionate as mine. We girls had been checking each other out in the gym changing room since grade five, when the early bloomers started budding. At eleven, I'd taken to wearing an AA-sized bra — its beige cups so barely visible it looked more like a gauze bandage than an actual brassiere — because a bra, any bra, attracted less negative attention than simply wearing an undershirt over my then-nonexistent breasts. I'd huddle in the corner of the changing room, shoulders curled protectively over my upper body as I pulled on my gym strip, hoping no one would notice my miniscule, asymmetrical chest.

As if being flat wasn't bad enough. In grade seven, the boys nicknamed me "Sec," as in Secretary of the Itty Bitty Titty Committee. Just the I.B.T.C., had been enough to elicit snickers: "Flat as a board and never been nailed!" My neighbour Johanne and my friend Colleen were dubbed "Pres" and "Vice," so at least I was in good company. But unlike me, their breasts, though small, actually matched. Two perfect little mounds rounding out their sweaters like pairs of identical twins.

At sixteen, my doctor probed and pressed my breasts in a circular motion, coaching me on how to perform a monthly self-exam. "If *this* doesn't change," she mused, waving her free hand at my mismatched, half-baked boobs, "you might want to consider silicone implants." This was the 80s and silicone was all the rage, even though no safety studies had yet been published and horror stories were beginning to emerge about leakage. I felt my entire body, naked and vulnerable, shrink behind the crinkly blue sheet. My doctor, my *feminist* doctor, the one who barely wore makeup, was telling me I might need a boob job? The same brainy young doctor with whom I'd had frank discussions about drugs and alcohol, contraception and sex, all the stuff I couldn't talk about with my parents? Wasn't she supposed to say things like, "bodies come in all sorts of shapes and sizes" and "you're okay just the way you are"? If I'd been a different kind of girl, I might have been relieved, elated even, to have my doctor's blessing to go under the knife. I might have skipped all the way to the plastic surgeon's. The stats are telling: by 1990, over one million American women and teenaged girls had undergone breast implant surgery. But in my doctor's office in the mid-'80s, all I felt was shame. All I could hear was *you are defective*.

Surgery was out of the question, anyway. As far as my girl-friends and I were concerned, boob jobs, like nose and ass jobs, were laughable, relegated to vain, vacuous glamour girls far away in LA. We were artsy misfits from drama club whose beauty regime consisted of excessive black eyeliner and hair gel to heighten and volumize our punky, New Wave do's. We hid our bodies under oversized sweatshirts and shaker-knit sweaters, worn off the shoulder à la Jennifer Beals in *Flashdance*. Besides, where was I going to come up with thousands of dollars for an elective cosmetic procedure? Money from babysitting and my part-time job at the library were hardly going to cut it. There was no way I was going to broach the topic with my parents. Even if it wasn't mortally embarrassing, my dad was stingy to a fault and my mom was always telling me to stop being so image conscious. And part of me knew she was right — *it shouldn't matter*. Except that it did.

Regardless, my under-developed, lopsided breasts were the least of my worries. They were just one of many indications that I wasn't normal. All my friends were dating boys, but I had crushes on girls. Was my skewed, practically androgynous chest yet another sign that I was a *lesbian*, a word that lurked in the corners of my teenaged consciousness but that I was too afraid to utter aloud?

＊＊

Ten years later, on the other side of the country, another doctor's office, another routine breast exam. My west coast GP palpated my mutant right breast, which had now sprouted a forest of unseemly, wiry hair around the nipple. "If *this* bothers you," she said cheerfully, "you can always go to the mastectomy clinic — for women with breast cancer? — and get fitted with a prosthetic."

Silicone implants were now out of vogue; they'd been banned by Health Canada in 1992 and wouldn't be back on the market until 2006. Like my hometown doctor, my new GP didn't give a name to *this*. Her suggestion, which seemed preposterous, further cemented my shame. I'd been trying to get over my body issues for years. "No woman is ever truly happy with her breasts," I'd read somewhere, which for a time had helped normalize my angst. In women's studies classes in undergrad, we'd examined how the media set artificial, unattainable beauty standards for women. But now, my new doctor was confirming my worst fears, the very thing I'd known way back in that Sears changing room with my mother. This wasn't just a case of me having poor body image; my breasts really were abnormal. So abnormal they needed fixing. It was one thing for airbrushed images in beauty magazines to tell me so; it was another for a succession of feminist doctors — educated women who saw countless ordinary breasts every single day — to corroborate this ugly truth.

Still, there was no way in hell I was going to take myself to the mastectomy clinic. "So, uh, my doc says you can fix me up with an appendage to fill out my bra?" Embarrassment aside, it just felt plain wrong. These prosthetics had been designed for women who'd had their breasts *amputated*, cancer patients who'd lost a part of themselves, never mind undergoing the hell of chemo and radiation. I hadn't lost anything. I just longed for something I'd never had.

I relayed this story to a trusted friend at work, who took me for a lunchtime shopping spree at LaSenza. I was pleasantly surprised by the selection — bra shopping had always been an ordeal. Bra manufacturers assumed if you were an A-cup, you were petite all over. Finding a 36A in those days, particularly in a style that was even remotely sexy, was next to impossible. Warner's Petites line for small breasts had saved me for a while, but then The Bay stopped carrying them. When I made enquiries as to why, the clerk gave me a withering look. "We have plenty of other bras," she snapped. "Get over it." She was about ten years older than me; thin, stylish and oozing attitude. No offer to help me find a suitable alternative, nothing. Ridiculously, I just stood there shaking with anger, willing myself not to cry. *Get over it?* When you have breasts like mine, there is no getting over it.

But here at LaSenza there was a cornucopia of sexy styles, pretty colours and fabrics, even in the lowly A-sizes. The sales staff was pleasant and discreet. This was long before the chain began hawking flannel jammies and tacky thongs for tweens; LaSenza of the '90s was Canada's answer to Victoria's Secret. The brand had developed its own custom padded push-up bra that cleverly disguised what was lacking with interior fabric side cushions you could insert or remove as needed for desired fullness. I tried on a style in soft, silky mauve with matching lace trim, and checked out my profile. My left side looked surprisingly curvy, but the right cup still sagged pathetically. The sales clerk hurried off and returned with an extra side cushion. I slid it into the right panel over the existing pad and suddenly, like magic, my chest was evenly rounded. Sure, it was just a step up from padding my bra with Kleenex, but it worked. For the first time in my life, I could put on a brassiere and actually feel sexy. I took home at least three styles that day, with matching panties.

Wearing my new lingerie under street clothes, I'd never felt more confident. But a key problem remained: what happened when the bra came off and my true, misshapen self was revealed? Just the thought of getting naked with someone terrified me. By this time, I was comfortably out as a dyke. The stakes were higher now; it mattered more that I be attractive to a potential lover. I couldn't just shrug off breast fixation as a male preoccupation as I had in university when I'd dated a guy whose roommate had a boob chart prominently displayed in the living room. This crass classification table, complete with cartoon illustrations and irreverent labels (Lemons, Mail Bags, Coat Hooks, Flapjacks, and so on), had provided endless hours of hilarity for the house full of raucous college boys. Now that I was openly queer, I had to admit that I, too, was genuinely attracted to a nice pair of boobs, and it pained me to know that I was sorely lacking in this department myself. How would another woman ever find me desirable? "You've got a set of Pointers," my university boyfriend had whispered more than once, referencing the infamous boob chart during foreplay, "cute little Pointers." Either love was blind, or he was being overly generous. While my left breast marginally passed as a mini-Pointer, the right was only a Bee Sting.

At Take Back the Night marches, I always hung back as fellow young dykes whipped off their shirts and paraded topless, a brazen F-you to the patriarchy we were railing against. Gwen Jacob's indecency charge was fresh in everyone's minds; the nineteen-year-old student had been arrested in Guelph, Ontario, in 1991 for having the gall to walk home topless on a sweltering July day. Under the glow of autumn streetlamps, the bare-breasted marchers seemed so empowered, so free, strutting down the yellow centre line of downtown streets after dark, showing off their tattoos and body piercings. Part of me longed to join them, but I knew that even in this body-positive crowd I would still attract stares. Feminists could sure talk the talk, but despite our best intentions, we didn't always walk the walk. I didn't want to be a freak show amidst my own sisters, my new dating pool.

It was in the LGBT community that I first encountered people who longed to get rid of their breasts altogether, from butches who concealed them under boyish clothes to trans folk who bound their chests while awaiting top surgery. Here were individuals endowed with the ample, perfectly matched boobs that I coveted, but these folks were just as distressed by their chests — in some cases, considerably more so — than I was. One of my earliest queer lovers, a slight, androgynous dyke with smaller tits than me (albeit, symmetrical), couldn't understand my newfound devotion to lingerie. She didn't wear a bra at all.

A decade later, just as same-sex marriage was legalized in Canada, I met Amanda, the woman who would become my wife. She fell for me at first glance, on account of my long legs and the dimple in my cheek when I smiled. By the time my shirt came off a couple of dates later, she didn't run away. She has a way with my breasts like no one else. Her own boobs are voluptuous, "too big," she complains, having flirted with the idea of reduction surgery. A tomboy who grew up into a butch, she never really wanted breasts — they weigh her down, make her back ache, get in the way when she's playing sports. Still, there's nothing I like better than pleasuring her girls or snuggling into her ample bosom.

When we got married, I had a wedding dress made to measure, a strapless, femmy number with a fitted bodice and a skirt that just skimmed the floor. The designer thoughtfully added some extra padding to the right cup. "You're planning on having kids?" she queried as she zipped me in at my final fitting. "When breastfeeding, be sure to favour your right nipple. That'll help even out your chest."

Silicone implants, prosthetics — and now *breastfeeding*? I really had heard it all. Then again, breastfeeding was all that really mattered. The entire evolutionary point of boobs, I reasoned. What did it matter if mine were cosmetically flawed, so long as they *worked*? I'd bought into the adage *every woman can breastfeed* since high school, when I'd done a project on the Nestlé baby formula scandal. I'd been shocked to discover that the hot chocolate associated with the warmth and comfort of my childhood was made by the same company killing babies in the third world with its infant formula. I'd passionately boycotted Nestlé, even though it meant giving up Kit Kat bars. Despite the chronic self-loathing I felt toward my breasts, there was no question that when the time came, I would breastfeed my baby.

But three days postpartum, my milk was nowhere in sight. My son had lost more than a third of his birth weight and was failing to thrive. I held my gaunt little baby to my breast, terrified I was going to lose him. His latch was good, I'd perfected the breastfeeding hold, but the white stuff just wasn't flowing. We'd gone from "feed on demand" to scheduled feeds every two hours, supplementing with donor breast milk through a cumbersome cup and feeding tube process. The tube, a tiny straw the size of a headphone wire, was taped to the tip of my overworked nipple. I got the baby to latch while Amanda painstakingly submerged the other end into a medicine cup filled with milk. The parts were hard to grasp, she had to get the angle just right for the milk to flow, but she couldn't let her fingers come in contact with the milk itself for fear of contamination. Her fingers shook from lack of sleep, but the donor milk was such a precious commodity we couldn't afford to spill a drop.

When we weren't feeding, Amanda and the baby slept while I pumped with the massive hospital breast pump, an ancient warhorse that looked and sounded like a cattle-milking machine. It was an exercise in futility. A few beads of moisture formed inside the clear plastic receptacle, but not a single drop was expressed from my breasts. Our midwives, who were closely monitoring the situation, reassured me that my shape and size had nothing to do with it, but I knew better: my small, mismatched breasts had let me down again, at a time when it mattered most.

In the pro-breastfeeding maternity ward there was no tolerance for failure. As our baby's weight plummeted, the nursing staff, so warm and friendly post-delivery, noticeably chilled. Every move we made was suddenly met with intense scrutiny. I finally asked one of our midwives what I'd been afraid to utter aloud: was it possible that I was one of those small percentage of women who

simply can't breastfeed? She considered carefully, clearly discon-
certed that I hadn't yet experienced any warmth in my boobs or
sensation of letdown. "I like to think it's possible for every woman, under the right circumstances and with the right support, to
breastfeed."

Bolstered by the midwife's unwavering faith, we kept at it,
the whole crazy, exhausting cup/tube/pumping dance, waiting
to strike liquid gold. On day five, the hospital lactation consultant
jumped up and down like a cheerleader when I finally expressed a
smattering of tiny white droplets with the pump. But it was just a
tease. By day seven, back at home and out of donor milk, we had
to switch to the formula I'd long abhorred. The crowning irony?
The only brand our son could tolerate was Good Start, made by
none other than Nestlé.

By this time, I was tube-feeding using a Supplemental Nursing System (SNS), an inverted, plastic bottle with an air vent that
hung from a string around my neck and nestled between my
breasts. Two feeding tubes ran down from the bottle and were
taped to the tip of each nipple. It looked like some bizarre fetish
get-up, but it meant I could nurse my baby by myself.

I tried everything: herbs with quaint names like fenugreek
and blessed thistle, nursing teas, homeopathics and even Domper-
idone, a prescription drug developed for prostate cancer whose
side effects include stimulating milk production. For the next five
weeks I was applauded by health providers for stubbornly stick-
ing to it, even long after it was reasonable or sane to do so. Our
midwives, baffled by my lack of progress, finally referred me to a
physician at the Vancouver Breastfeeding Centre. The specialist
took one look at my naked chest and proclaimed in her no-nonsense British accent: "I've seen breasts like yours before. There's
not much hope for you, I'm afraid."

She supervised a feed anyway, just to be sure, a timed feed
at my breast without the SNS, weighing my son before and after
so she could calculate what, if anything, he was getting from me
without the formula. The figures confirmed her worst suspicions —
during the five-minute test, I'd produced less than half a teaspoonful

of milk. I was officially diagnosed with lactation failure. So much for *every woman can breastfeed*.

"You have a condition called breast hypoplasia," she announced. "A rare physical defect." I didn't have enough glandular tissue to store milk; my breasts hadn't developed properly during puberty, and there was nothing we could do to reverse this. After all these years, finally, I had a diagnosis. "I could keep making you work very hard at breastfeeding," she said, "but there's no point. I don't mean to sound harsh, but that's why formula was invented. To save babies like yours."

The embarrassment I'd long experienced around my boobs was nothing compared to the shaming I endured formula-feeding my baby. Every time I pulled out a bottle, I was met with disapproving stares from strangers. The moms from stroller fit stopped talking to me altogether after I bottle-fed in class. There was no opportunity to explain, *this isn't my choice; I'd rather be breastfeeding*.

None of my breastfeeding books even mentioned hypoplasia. Inadequate milk supply was blamed on everything from not feeding long enough, not pumping enough, not drinking enough water, not eating right, not getting enough sleep (seriously, what new mother is getting enough sleep?), to being distracted by too many visitors. *Only a negligible percentage of women truly cannot breastfeed due to underlying medical conditions*, the books noted without elaboration, not wanting to grant struggling mothers an exit clause. My sister-in-law, who meticulously researches everything, emailed a couple of articles on breast hypoplasia, the scant few she'd managed to track down in medical journals. As I flipped through a study published in *Pediatrics* in the mid-'80s, my eyes landed on a photo of breasts that looked eerily familiar, tiny and asymmetrical, more tubular than round. No wonder the breastfeeding specialist had known right away. I'd never before seen another set of boobs like mine, but there they were — mini, off-kilter Pointers.

My own Google search at the time yielded four meagre hits. A medical definition noted that hypoplasia is one of the few conditions that legitimately warrant breast augmentation surgery. I sat at my laptop, stunned. My hometown doctor had been right on the mark after all. What was it about *me*, then, that had prevented me from getting surgery all these years? Pride? Fear of mockery, of painful, debilitating side effects, of cancer? Somewhere deep inside, some part of me still clung to the belief that physical appearance shouldn't matter — that I was okay, beautiful even, just the way I was, even if I didn't always feel it. It didn't make sense, though: if I were to lose a tooth or a limb, or be suddenly disfigured, I would get corrective surgery in a heartbeat. I regularly coloured my hair and shaped my eyebrows; I'd even worn braces as a kid to fix my overbite. Why were my breasts so different? I had to honestly ask myself: If I were sixteen and could do it all over again knowing what I know now, would I get a boob job?

Maybe.

⚑⚐

I'd like to say I've finally made peace with my breasts, but that would be a lie. A grudging acceptance is more accurate. I'm still self-conscious sometimes — going for a mammogram or working out at the pool (athletic bathing suits are so unforgiving!) — but advances in bra design mean I can mostly pass as normal. I have a wife who loves me and finds me sexy, even after eleven years. I have a school-aged son who is healthy, happy and blazingly bright, despite being reared on formula. Really, what more could I want?

I recently stumbled upon a contemporary boob chart by New York animator Lessa Millet, "a scientific look at woman's greatest accessory," on Slutever.com. Millet's table, with its tasteful, whimsical line drawings and clever, tongue-in-cheek labels effectively reimagines and reclaims the frat boy boob chart. Amidst The Kisses, The Freelancers, and The Mad Men, I was pleasantly surprised to find an accurate representation of myself: The Variety Pack. The artfully simple, cheery depiction of my mismatched breasts makes me smile.

I've also been back to the lingerie section at The Bay. I was emergency shopping for a replacement strapless — I was due at a swanky party in a matter of hours — and as I scoured the racks,

I found myself flooded with familiar dread. Despite the dizzying selection of styles, brands and colours, I couldn't find anything remotely appropriate in my size. I felt like a teenager all over again, reduced to tears in that changing room with my mother. A sales clerk spotted me floundering and offered her help. "You're in luck," she said. "I'm a professional bra fitter and I've just come on shift. Let's go to a fitting room and I'll give you a measure."

"I have a physical defect called breast hypoplasia," I informed her as she wrapped her tape around my bustline. It felt infinitely better to have words now, a name for *this*.

"I can see your challenge," she concurred sympathetically. "But you've got your size right. Thirty-six-A is appropriate for your left breast. It's just a matter of finding the right style to enhance your smaller breast. Let me go look."

I stood there in the small cubicle, topless and shivering, growing increasingly anxious as I waited. She was taking a long time — would I be the one client she couldn't help? She finally came back with a startling array of choices in both regular and strapless styles. "Just try them all on so we can get a sense of what works."

I slipped on a simple black bra by Maidenform and adjusted the straps. The material was a new synthetic, sleek and luxuriously soft against my delicate skin. It was an everyday style, nothing special, but it instantly transformed my chest without finicky pads or pumps.

"Wow," was all I could manage as I looked at myself in the mirror. "Thank you."

"You're welcome." She beamed. "Every woman deserves to look and feel beautiful."

Bump

Rebecca Hendry

You find it when you're lying on your couch watching *Midnight in Paris*. The wire from your bra is digging into your left side so you unhook it, reach through the arm of your T-shirt to pull the strap through. As your fingers brush the skin to release the fabric from your breast, you feel it.

A little bump.

You press into it, trace it with your fingertips. It's round and smooth, the size of a jellybean. It's close to the surface and moves when you push it. Fear swirls through your belly and radiates out, the movie forgotten, every familiar thing in your living room fading from view as you laser in on this tiny thing you know does not belong.

You climb the stairs to your bedroom, your bra half off, the strap dangling from your shirt sleeve. At your desk you Google "smooth, round lump in breast." The results are not reassuring.

This is how it starts, you think. For some women, this is exactly how it starts.

❧

The doctor has to ask you three times where it is. She prods and pushes, but it keeps sliding out of the way. You find it and hold the spot with your finger. You have become very familiar, you and this bump. You check it several times a day. Is it harder? Softer? Was it always that big? That small?

"Ah," she says when she finds it. She gazes at a point on the wall above your head, concentrating, as though listening to classical music and trying to pick up the subtleties. "That feels like a lymph node," she says. "I'm not too worried about it. It should be gone within a few weeks. But come back if it's not."

At home you Google "lymph node under left arm." You don't like what you find.

⚛

You wait seven weeks for your little bump to go away. You give yourself extra time because bodies are mysterious, and a lymph node could be swollen for lots of reasons. But it's still there every time you check, sliding beneath your fingers like a small fish.

Your doctor books you for a mammogram. "Don't worry," she says. "It's rare for a lump like that to turn out to be anything." But worry has taken up residence. It flares up as you go about your day, sometimes paralyzing you before retreating again. You're a single mother with no insurance. What if...

You don't talk about the bump to your children, your friends or family, the new man you're seeing. You hide your fear well. That's always been your way. Someone once told you that you should be a paramedic, a doctor. Someone who stays calm in emergencies. You're always so calm, she had said.

But you're not calm at all. You're worried if you tell other people the worry will spread, metastasize and take you over completely.

⚛

The mammogram technician asks you where it is. You show her and she marks it with a small sticker with a round metal bead in the centre so the radiologist can find the bump easily. She presses your breast in a clear plastic vise and tells you to hold your breath. She lowers the vise, squeezes your breast until the pain makes the floor waver beneath you, then releases it. She says she will be back to tell you if the radiologist recommends the ultrasound. You wait, your bare back cold against the plastic chair, your pale blue gown bunched around your lap.

She returns to tell you that, based on what he saw, he would like you to have the ultrasound.

You wonder if they practise this sunny warmth, if it's hard for them after so many of the wrong kind of lumps, so many hopeful women searching their faces for clues to their survival. You sense nothing from the blank-faced woman.

You nod, wonder for the first time if you should have brought someone with you. If they find something, this could be when you find out. Will you be able to drive yourself home knowing? You imagine somehow that the earth will open beneath you, that the terror will split you in half. Will you be able to stop for butter and milk and sandwich bags, make your children the homemade mac and cheese you were planning for dinner?

The ultrasound tech is an acquaintance you are fond of. She smiles and jokes while she peers at her screen and glides the sticky wand over your skin, but then she is silent. You can pick up something, some subtle signal she's emitting, and watch her face, the screen, but you don't know what any of it means. Everything looks dangerous, every black spot, squiggly line, round grey circle looks deadly.

When she's done she says the radiologist will want to look at a couple of areas. She seems apologetic. She doesn't joke any-more. When she returns she tells you the radiologist has recom-mended a biopsy. The earliest appointment she can get is ten days away. "It's the best I can do," she says. You feel like you're falling, slipping through the cold metal bed.

❧

It's summer, so you do summer things while you're waiting. You go camping with the kids, have dinners with your friends, hike, work on writing projects. When you talk to your mother in Toron-to you don't mention it. One friend knows, and as soon as you tell her you wish you could pull the tendril back before the fear takes root in her as well.

At night, when you're alone, you Google biopsy statistics. You read that 80 percent of breast lump biopsies are benign, but percentages mean nothing to you. You know of parents who have lost more than one child to separate freak accidents. A child who lost both parents in one year to sudden, rampaging cancer. A woman who was the sole survivor of a plane crash that killed six people and then went on to die in another plane crash five years later.

It works the other way, too, with good things. What are the chances of winning the lottery? Not good. Except… one time when you wanted to take your kids to Disneyland you won $2,700 in Lotto 649, the exact price for the trip. What are the chances? Slim to none.

But still.

❦

You're back in the pale blue gown at the hospital, surrounded by other women in pale blue gowns leafing through gardening magazines. The friend who knows sends you a text, probably saying something kind and supportive, but you don't read it. You wish you hadn't told her, you wish nobody knew at all, you wish you were completely and utterly alone.

You wish you didn't have to think about the other blue-gowned women and their secret bumps, wonder which ones will make it and which ones won't. One of them has a partner with her. You watch him talk to her gently, pick up her sock when it falls from her lap, and something stirs in you. He's in it, you think. He's in it with her. What is that like, you wonder. Does it help her, or just make her more afraid? When she is called to go in, he tells her he will be right there waiting for her.

❦

The radiologist tells you that once they're set up it should only take five minutes. But she has underestimated your slippery bump, that sassy little fish. They freeze the top of your breast with local anesthetic while you lie on your side. The biopsy needle is impossibly long and impossibly thick. You can't feel the pain, only the pressure, but imagine the tearing and ripping of tissue and muscle until you tell yourself to stop.

You lose count of her attempts as you watch the ultrasound screen. The tip of the needle slips off the surface of the bump, bouncing away from it each time. She tries again and again, pressing deep into you with her hand to stabilize the breast.

At one point your phone rings from your purse under the hospital bed. "Is it important?" the radiologist asks, needle hovering in hand. You tell her it's probably your son, home alone and wondering if he's allowed to make toast or watch TV. "Does he know you're here?" she asks. You shake your head.

Forty-five minutes later they are done, after trying from two different directions with two different kinds of needle. The tech has placed a cold cloth on your head because she said you looked queasy. You're dizzy. You should have eaten something before you came.

At home under the bathroom lights your breast is turning purplish black and yellow, the bruise already the size of your hand. One puncture wound is covered in a small, blood-soaked bandage you are too squeamish to remove, the other is bare but leaking tiny rosebud drops onto your loose tank top. You look like you have been beaten, how you imagine a beaten woman looks.

When the children aren't looking, you sneak the small square ice pack the ultrasound tech gave you from the freezer and slide it breathlessly into your bra. You take the kids out, buy them sushi, help them choose an appropriate movie. You make yourself rice and vegetables, think about the benefits of fresh ground ginger, crushed garlic, but also — you can't help it — wonder if it's too late.

Thoughts flutter through your mind about where your children would live. There is not a single option you feel at peace with. And who would go through your belongings? You imagine your group of book club girls sorting papers in your basement, old report cards, letters from your grandmother, photos. Deciding what matters and what doesn't. The meaning, the nostalgia of your entire life on this earth utterly lost on them.

You want to go to bed, hold your battered breast like an injured bird against you. You want to tell it you're sorry. You want someone to run you a bath, bring you tea, but still you will not pick up the phone.

While the kids are at their dad's, you go watch a movie with the man you are seeing casually. After ten years of being entwined in a passionately dysfunctional marriage, you struggle to understand the concept of casual in relation to men, but you think it can be defined by the fact that it doesn't occur to you to tell him you're afraid, every second now, that you might be dying. You laugh and drink wine, your breast bandaged and bruised under your bra.

When you get home there is a message from the doctor's office to come in and review your results the next day. It was supposed to take ten days. It has only been two. You have no idea whether this is good or bad.

You have run out of things to look up on the internet. You eat Coconut Bliss ice cream, watch a zombie movie.

At a loss, you Google "do I have cancer?"

❧

That night you don't sleep. Instead, you lie there and you think about all the people in your life. You're not sure why. You think about people you used to know but don't talk to anymore, people you have pushed aside, people who have hurt you. Now you wonder, was anything they did really that bad?

You think, who do I care about? It suddenly seems important.

Who do you worry about when you're driving to work? Who can make you cry on your bathroom floor like a teenage girl, whose tiny, fluttering eyelids have you traced with a sleepy finger in the moonlight? Whose breath did you count to lull yourself to sleep, *one... two... three*. Which friends can you laugh with, make barefoot summer meals with, sing with? Who do you want to hug, shake, shout at because they terrify you, because you love them, because you could lose them with one car going a little too fast, one red pumping heart that just decides to stop, one tiny bump.

You think of the man waiting for his blue-gowned wife.

Who's in this with me, you wonder. Who's here? Maybe it does help after all, what do you know? You aren't sure, but maybe it does. You tell yourself they would fight for you if you asked them to. This army of your beloved.

From Scar to Sacrament

Heidi Grogan

My left scar starts at my armpit and makes a softly convex curve. My right scar runs mid-breast in a more discreet location, as far as bathing suits and tank tops go.

The surgeon expressed regret that they do not match. But I like them this way. The design is original, like a tribal marking of a rite of passage. After the mastectomy the left scar was thick and tough to look at. The reconstruction surgeon said, "This will never do," and now both scars are pencil thin, with tiny red blood vessels showing at the sides as they valiantly work to heal the area. Soon they will be nearly invisible silver lines, with tattooed nipples sitting above them — together looking like the balance points under scar-scales of justice. Then my children will breathe a sigh of relief that all is well, and they'll say that Terry Fox gave our family a great gift. My seven-year-old son thinks that before Terry, everyone with cancer died.

There is a psychology of scars. A wound is not a scar until the skin has healed completely. Living with a scar affects a whole family. Emotional wounds form scars too, as a sign of healing. My physical and psychic wounds put distance between me and my family because they are ugly to me. They look ugly. They make me feel ugly. They match.

My sister-in-law Cheryl came to the hospital to offer support when it was time to remove the bandages. The first look at the damage. The nurse poked her head through the curtain circling my bed, asked me where I wanted to do this. I said let's do it in the bathroom, there is a mirror there, places to sit. Two older men shared the four-bed hospital room. One was dying and the other was grumpy. My third roommate was a woman who also had a mastectomy. They didn't need to be part of the unveiling. The three of us — the nurse, Cheryl and I — shuffled around the tight spaces of the bed and the beige privacy curtain, past the brown tray with green jello and strong tea, past the vase of double-blooming blush tulips and blue hyacinth. We closed the bathroom door behind us, faced the mirror.

The nurse said it looked good as she kept unwrapping. A little reaction to the tape here, she said, so I'm peeling slowly. Cheryl placed her hand on my shoulder. The bandage was off now and I looked up at her. Our eyes locked in the mirror, and we both looked down. My God. I laid my palm on the rubbery skin covering my ribs from my armpit to my remaining breast: no mound, no pink centre. There was no nipple, just a vast area of flat. The red slash, puckered where stitches leaked amber pus, marked the surgeon's trail. I looked away, sought the safety of Cheryl's face.

Cheryl paled, her eyes travelling the barren ground of my chest. I could tell she was biting the inside of her cheek. She looked to the side, away from me, and I thought *Oh she's sad, she's thinking Crap this is hard*. Then I saw her eyes roll up in her head, only the whites showing. My mouth froze in a silent "Oh no" as the nurse kept picking at the tape and Cheryl fell straight back, hard against the bathroom door, her head making a loud crack as she slid to the floor. She slumped forward awkwardly with her chin tucked to her chest. The nurse scrambled to cradle her head, reached for the emergency help cord by the toilet. She didn't want to let her go and couldn't reach. Opened the door and yelled, "WE NEED SOME HELP IN HERE!" So the old man, not the grumpy one, and the other mastectomy lady who was not supposed to be moving her arms, both attempted to crawl out of their beds and the nurse yelled, "NO, NOT YOU! I NEED A DOCTOR IN HERE!" Cheryl began to make breathing noises, somewhere between a snore and a gasp, then snapped her head up and looked around. She was still out, her eyes blank.

Later, Cheryl lying on my hospital bed, the nurse checked her blood pressure and her pupils. Cheryl was mortified. "Was it so bad?" I said.

"It was the grief." Her fingertips pressed lightly on mine. "It was just that it was gone, and all that was left was a scar that looked like a deforested clear-cut site."

In the first weeks after the surgery I could not touch the skin around the tender red scar. My daughter, Abby, rubbed cream onto the scar, with tiny three-year-old hands, asking, head tilted to one side, when the doctor would make me "a new boob."

Later that summer we went camping. One morning, just as the sun hit the eastern peak of our tent, shining a soft orange light into the tent, I felt my son, Aidan, shift inside his sleeping bag. As agreed in whispers the night before, we dressed quietly for our secret fishing mission. There was no room for discretion in the tent's small space, and when I pulled on my fleece sweater Aidan gaped. "Wow! That doctor really *did* take your whole boob off!"

In September, I lost the remaining breast. Abby asked me if she was going to have to get a new mother. Aidan looked after me, cradling my head in the crook of his arm when we lay down to talk at bedtime; my little man. Mike and I were tired, and went through the motions without the adrenalin because we knew how it worked this time. After that surgery, I didn't think about ugly; it was easy to override that reality with gratitude for being alive. And I didn't want reconstruction... didn't want to be Barbie. I felt stupid, self-conscious at the idea of getting a new and customized rack. Yet, my kids had the idea I would only be well when I had new breasts.

I booked the reconstruction surgery, but secretly dreaded it. I sat on our green couch, making recovery plans: the logistics of time off work, childcare, the details that kept me focused. My husband, Mike, turned off the TV, cutting off *Survivor*'s Jeff in mid-sentence at Tribal Council. He reached for my hand. "I don't think you should do it."

This was the man who bought new sheets for our bed before I came home breastless, gently closed the bedroom door so I could sleep with my arm propped on pillows while he made our suppers, did our laundry. He'd cried when I cried, assuring me he was grateful for the scars as reminders that our family would survive. But I knew the nipple-less flat of my ribs also reminded him of how close he had come to being the only parent. He hadn't needed to say a word; I felt the hesitation in his touch, and I understood, for touching the red bumpy scar running over my ribs made it too real to bear. For Mike, as for Abby and Aidan, new breasts would be a sign that all would be well. So, what the hell was he talking about? Don't do it?

"I think you should go see someone, a counsellor."

"I'm fine with it," I said. "I am happy to do this, for the kids." *For you*, was unspoken. We were still not able to name the fear out loud. "Everyone will feel better."

He shook his head. "That won't be a good enough reason. I mean for you, later."

I knew he was right, and we were quiet. I needed to find out why I was resistant. I was more terrified about reconstruction than I'd been about mastectomy. Why?

❦

The doctor I am seeing today counsels breast cancer patients. I had made and cancelled the appointment twice. This third time, as I sat waiting for her, I fought the urge to put on my coat and leave. She was late. I had things to do. I focused on the knick-knacks in her office. There were several of the "angels of courage" that Hallmark sells — they are the colour of biscuits fresh from the oven, angels standing with their arms held high in victory. I still couldn't hold my arm over my head like that. When you have breast cancer, you get a lot of those angels. Aidan rearranges mine regularly, making "scenes" throughout the house. Over Christmas, they got to hang out with Mary and Joseph and the shepherds in the nativity scene on top of our wine cabinet; the holy family (along with a stuffed Santa) hung over the eaves of the stable looking at Jesus upside down.

Then the doctor came in; tall, curly black hair, bold paisley skirt. She shook my hand, sat down and asked why I was there, how she could help. Blood rushed to my face. I wiped my sweaty hands on my jeans. I told her I was struggling. I wanted my family to be comforted, but I had terrible anxiety about the reconstruction and I told her about Mike saying that it was great and noble to have surgery to close the gap of fear in our family, but that it was not a good enough reason to do it and that I thought he was right but didn't know why. I said this all in one long run-on sentence. Once it was out, I felt my tension drain away.

She asked me to talk about my reasons for resisting. "Philosophically, is there a problem?"

Yes. There sure is. I started through my list of reasons reconstruction is wrong: the $10K this would probably cost would be a nice gift to the Calgary Food Bank or a down payment for low-cost housing. The doctor reminded me that we live in Canada, that our value system supports treatment for those who have suffered what is essentially an amputation. I dismissed this as indulgent. That rationale didn't work, I told her. I wanted to defer my portion of the taxpayers' gift to the charity of my choice. A breast is not an essential body part. It is not like losing a hand or a leg. Breast reconstruction is not about function — it is about beauty.

"Ah," she said, and leaned forward, nodding. She drummed her long fingers on the arms of her chair. I said nothing. Embarrassed, because I was not born with a big chest. After the mastectomies, people had asked me what size I would choose for my new breasts, as though this was my chance to pick the size that would have looked better on me all along. I laughed, and when I was alone, I cried. That decision was a no-win. If I picked the size I'd been, then I'd be a martyr-loser. If I picked something bigger then I'd be admitting that I was ugly before, and I'd also be telling God He didn't do me justice when He put me together. Telling my Higher Power that the creation plan idea for me sucked is enough to put me in counselling for the next ten years. Just thinking about it in that office, I felt the fine hairs on the nape of my neck stand up. I couldn't speak any of this to the doctor, and the lump in my throat made it hard to swallow.

All of a sudden she started talking about Bible stories. What the hell? But I listened. Her stories were about women named Mary pouring expensive perfume onto Jesus's feet. I remembered there were a few of them. The doctor leaned forward and said that in one of the stories Mary came weeping, began wetting His feet with her tears, kept wiping them with her long hair, kissing and anointing them with perfume. She was a woman with a past, who had a lot to cry over. I'd always liked her story because I thought she was bold to show up among people who wanted nothing to do with her. The doctor wrapped it up saying Jesus doesn't push her away. I'd never thought about how Mary felt, had just read the story and thought *Yeah she's bold*. Now, I imagined what it was like to be Mary: time to stand up and leave the awkward scene. And I realized I was like her, feeling ugly, full to overflowing with fear and exhaustion — in need of a good cry. My eyes began to leak, and I wiped them with the backs of my wrists.

The doctor handed me a tissue, and adjusted the Courage Angel who stood beside the new white puff of surrender waving from the Kleenex box on the coffee table beside her. She kept talking.

Another Jesus story. Mary comes to the table where Jesus and her brother, Lazarus, are eating dinner only hours after Jesus raised Lazarus from the dead.

Nothing like a good meal after a hard day's work, I thought, and blew my nose.

"Is this the one where people tell her she's an idiot for wasting the money on perfume?"

The doctor nodded. I remember this one too. When Mary is criticized by the men standing around them for being excessive, Jesus says, "Leave her alone." I relate to the men, who would likely agree that paying for reconstruction is excessive. Should I walk by poor people with my new body while they wish for something to eat?

I work at a street agency where women whose bodies have been beaten and used in prostitution come to recover and reconstruct their lives. They live on $426 a month after rent and bus pass. They agree to say goodbye to all their street friends. They are poor and lonely, but agree to the rule because they know the lifestyle of the old friends will kill them. Not so different than my diseased breasts; I'd said goodbye to them no problem. I hadn't cared about reconstruction because it reeked like regret. I didn't regret the loss.

I told the doctor that I could relate to the people criticizing Mary. The idea of reconstruction made me feel uncomfortable, self-conscious, embarrassed and foolish. It felt indulgent. I live in a country where a mastectomy can happen fast enough to ensure my life continues, and carries no price tag or burden at all. But allowing taxpayers to cover the cost of reconstructing my body? Is my appearance more important than a hungry family with no home?

She said Mike was right, that by insisting on being noble, I was missing what was going on here for me. Personally.

"What do you mean?"

"Mary was anointing feet that would soon bear scars." I shook my head. She explained the timing; Jesus's physical wounding, His own personal nightmare, began shortly after this.

"Mary is extravagant," the doctor said, "pouring expensive perfume onto His feet, wiping them with her hair. The way the story ends, the whole house was filled with fragrance." She looked at me hard when she said this last part. Whispered how He would have smelled it in His suffering, when He was dying.

I sat up, alert.

"I have no idea what your wounds are." Her voice was soft, but not hesitant. "But physical wounding and life wounds are sometimes connected. And," she spoke slowly, "grief is like a string of Christmas tree lights — when we are hurt, the old wounds we thought we'd dealt with all light up again."

I nod. Can't speak.

"Perhaps your resistance to reconstruction has nothing to do with breast cancer. Or with the reality of poverty. Perhaps reconstruction is a gift God desires to give you, here at the physical place of your wounding." She was quiet. I felt too hot in this office, closed my eyes. I knew she was right. Pictured my chest: no nipple makes for an alien-looking body. But a practical one because I never needed a nipple: Abby and Aidan are adopted.

I experience motherhood as a deep grace. That I did not nurse Aidan and Abby and feel their tiny bodies filling with sustenance from my body makes the gift of being chosen by their birth mothers to be their mother that much more precious. My breasts did nothing to make me functional as a woman. Maybe the doctor was onto something; maybe a breastless body was a comfortable outcome for me, my body telling the truth. I did not create life. Reconstruction by default then was an uncomfortable outcome because I had not reconciled what my breasts were *for* in this life. I touched the scar resting flat on my ribs.

I told the doctor how embarrassed I'd been when friends insisted I could breastfeed my adopted babies using a lactation aid. They'd encouraged me to try this, saying it was a way to experience the full magic of motherhood. All I could picture was the tubing taped to my small empty breasts. I declined. The doctor nodded at the image, but I didn't stop talking. I was getting an idea.

I asked her if she had heard of Catherine of Siena, a fourteenth-century woman from Italy, my favourite mystic. She shook her head.

I explained that Catherine's spirituality was gory and graphic compared to today's neat and tidy religion; she insisted that the open wounds produced by the spear in Jesus's side allow us to come in and be nourished near His heart.

"Catherine even called the blood from His side mother's milk," I said. "People in those days thought that when mothers stopped menstruating after childbirth, their blood was re-channelled through the body and converted into milk."

I waited for her reaction to the idea that Jesus is like a mother, expressing love like milk from the site of His wound.

The doctor picked up the Courage Angel. "I suspect Catherine and Mary would have understood your predicament. Brokenness and hope reside together at scar-sites."

Energy flooded through me.

I put my hands on the edge of my chair, pushed up to stand and reached behind me to get my arms into my coat.

The doctor shook her head. "Where are you going?"

"I get it now," I told her. She'd said the right things. Not at all what I'd expected, but the right things.

—⊷—

I allowed the surgeon to build me a new body. Reconstruction was not a slap in the face of my Creator. Instead, I see the maternal nature of God present at the place I have been hurt, on these thin red lines. And, I see that like Mary's perfume filling the whole house when it was poured on feet about to be scarred, my scars represent a gift that goes beyond the original gift of continuing my life. I see my family gather close, relax in my presence. My children now rest their head on my chest comfortably. I look in the mirror and don't see Barbie, or a fake rack, but an outward expression of how I feel inside. Beautiful. Whole.

I am back on the green couch, and Abby wants me to read her a story. She leans her small shoulder and head into my chest, and it is soft. No longer a line of washboard ribs. This is wonderful. I read to her of girls who go through dark forests, fall asleep for years on end, prick their fingers, let down their hair. They are all wounded in some way, all unjustly so, and somehow they retain their human dignity. We move on to the emperor who has no clothes, where everything is fine and dandy so it seems, but Abby giggles the whole way through, knowing he looks ridiculous. Life is a divine tragedy. I recognize, for the first time in these stories, opportunities for seeing our wounds as sacraments, signs of transformation, inner healing and beauty restored.

There is a spirituality of scars. In fairy tales and in Greek myths, the hero who survives abandonment, trickery or betrayal is always wounded. I slip my hand inside my shirt, touch the raised scars running down across my chest and am glad. They are symbols of how my unjust wounds became sacred, a sacrament of divine presence right where it hurt. The fairy tales I have lived by are the same as the Jesus stories, Mary stories, and the stories of the women I work with, and Catherine the mystic. They tell me we all will be wounded and I must be wounded. It is what I do with the wounds that makes all the difference.

My scars transform me. Here, at the thin red lines, I experience mercy in their insistence that love is present at the site of wounding.

Note: Some names and identifying details have been changed to protect personal privacy.

Previously published in *Room Magazine*, 3.4 issue, (Vancouver: 2010)

Mirror Mirror on the Wall

Heidi Grogan

In the waiting room of Calgary's Foothills Hospital outpatient clinic, I feel a little like the protagonist in a fairy tale who has battled the monster but still has a long way before she's out of the woods. I look around at my surroundings. Three Mennonite women squish onto a plush bench-seat. Round faces, wire-rim spectacles atop rosy cheeks. Black skirts with white stripes like the lines separating asphalt from its less-safe shoulder, running from their hems to mid-thigh. Blouses a dark purple paisley, collars tight to their necks. Black kerchiefs tied under their chins, black with big white polka dots. The woman on the left end of the bench has a wrinkled, fleshy face; the one on the right end is thirty-something and the girl between them looks to be about fourteen — three generations of thick-bodied women. I get up from my seat. I want to pee before my name gets called. Coming out of the public bathroom is another Mennonite woman. She has a waist, and her hair is pulled up under her polka-dot kerchief, her cheekbones are high; she is sultry despite her outward trappings. She does not smile, and pushes past me. This one, she's not like the others. If I liked my body like I bet she likes hers, I'd be dismayed by the community uniform, so unflattering and unfeminine. Personally, I would have liked wearing dresses like that, could have hid in them.

I sink back down in the waiting-room chair, this time across from an old woman talking to a fortyish man with a shaved head and light stubble. He seems sinister — maybe it's the dark eyes. I turn away when he catches me staring. When I check again, he smiles — a completely different look. He hoists himself onto his crutches and moves through the crowded waiting room sideways, asks the triage nurse something, and shuffles back to the seat beside his old mother where they eat pitas from her daypack. They

46

are smiling away, talking with their mouths full and dropping lettuce, ham and red onion onto their laps and the floor. I cross my arms in front of my chest, tuck my fingers under my armpits and press my breasts together. Beneath my sweatshirt, the bags of silicone gel squish under mastectomy scars. The doctors explained the implants as pita pockets slipped in between the muscles.

My turn. I walk through the swinging doors labelled Out Patient Minor Surgery. Minor. "Let's cut you some new nipples and see if you still think it's minor," I say under my breath.

There are no enclosed patient rooms, just a long hallway and makeshift rooms. In my curtained-off space, it's standard routine: upper body clothes off, put on the folded blue gown set out for me on the paper-covered bed. I lie flat on the bed, tilt my chin down and see the mound of my nipple-less breasts under the gown. Look to my feet, and realize there is a hole in my sock. Crap! Before I left the house I changed my new Christmas socks with their reindeer and candy canes for these that look better with black pants. I can't look like a dork; I'm getting new nipples. Too late, I realize these socks are worn through on the bottoms, threadbare. Despite the privacy of this mortifying discovery, I feel my face redden. When the nurse named Gail comes to tuck the warm sheet around my legs, I point my feet so she can't see my soles.

"Dr. DeNayer will be here in a moment," she assures me. Gail leaves, and the curtains swing closed behind her. The green surgical sheets that will cover me lie folded on silver trays with lids polished to gleaming. Like chafing dishes at a gourmet buffet. I decide I don't want to lie here for who knows how long, waiting for the doctor. I get up, stretch and notice that the sheets were sterilized this morning, according to the tape across the top. Like a "best before 11jan09." Blue plastic bins line up on shelves stacked floor to ceiling along the long wall. I wander over and read the labels: rectal tote, circumcision tote, gyne tote, eye tote, tote for drains, catheters and feeding tubes, tote for screwdrivers, pliers and saws. On the bottom right shelf is the breast implant tote — I know what's in that one. I flinch at the possible reasons for yanking the rectal tote from its shelf, contents opened by Gail for some poor sucker lying on this paper-covered bed.

Doctor DeNayer comes in with Nurse Gail following right behind.

"Must be pretty bad for the guy you have to use this stuff on," I say, and point to the rectal tote.

He gets a look, part grimace and part professional, furrowing his eyebrows in a remembering kind of way. Nods. Checks the silver tray of surgical tools, and surprises me by saying, "What's a tote-bin anyway — it's not a word."

I raise my eyebrows at him. "It's a bin with everything you need in it, like a tote bag."

Gail says, "You know, tote, like tote something around in a tote bag."

"Tote bag is not a word," he says. He scrubs his hands at the sink.

"It is." I say this, and Gail agrees.

A young doctor comes through the curtains, listens to this absurd conversation and says, "Tote is an adjective to bag." De-Nayer introduces him to me as the new resident doctor doing his rotation in plastic surgery.

"No, it's a noun," I say.

"And a verb," says Gail.

DeNayer says he dislikes words that are used incorrectly, like functionality. Function does well in every sentence where functionality is used. I reach inside my gown: my pretend-breasts do not function. They have no ducts to hold milk, and no nipples to secrete milk. Their mammary functionality is non-existent.

"Like causality," I say. He smiles as he inspects the surgical tools Gail has laid out on the buffet trays.

"I'm going to Google the definition of tote bag," says Gail. DeNayer lifts his head, says she'll have to rescrub to come back in, and she says, "Oh well, I'm looking it up."

She returns a minute later, says tote was first used in the 1900s and is a noun. DeNayer shakes his head. He is ready now, his equipment checked and tote taken care of. He asks if I have thought about where I want the nipples. *Yeah,* I think to myself, *I thought they'd look good where they originally were before we lopped everything off.*

"No, you do it." I figure he's done this enough times to know what won't look stupid. I let my mind wander: my friend tried to help me prepare for today, had showed up at my office at work, hauled me into the bathroom, coloured felt pens poking out of their pockets. She'd whipped off her shirt, bugged me til I did too. I picture us there, standing in front of the mirror, the hand towels with their yellow embroidered flowers in the reflection behind us. Sheena and I, shoulder to shoulder, same height, her breasts unscarred, and barely telling of their function for her two kids. Mine, by their perfect slope, announcing themselves as replacements of the original ones that never nursed anyone, their uselessness confirmed by cancer. She'd taken her finger and drawn an imaginary line from her nipple to her collar bone. "See where it's centered?" she'd said. I'd rolled my eyes, let her draw the imaginary lines on me. Then she'd pulled the pens from her pocket, marked perfect red circles and turned them into suns with little rays in orange and yellow.

❦

DeNayer, the resident, and I go into another room. The three of us stand with our faces reflecting back in a tiny blue plastic-framed mirror. Faces and my open blue gown. I think how funny this is, me and two men I hardly know, deciding where my nipples should be. It's not weird. It should be. But they've got this non-sexual yet totally interested attentiveness, and standing between them, I feel safe. More than safe. Like a work of art in the early stages. I feel like crying. Seems like this would have been a good way to feel all my life. I blame too many people, circumstances beyond my control, for interfering with my canvas. Bad apples. Flawed genetics. Myself, for being victim-ugly. Witches and wolves, because they interfered with my canvas and ruined everything.

These two, they're nothing like the wolves I grew up fearing in fairy tales. They look at me with interest, like they are envisioning

49

what could be. I trust them because I don't see much potential here at all. In the hospital light my chest looks like it is adorned with matching dollar-store Easter eggs — the plastic kind that come apart for parents to fill with treats.

I loved Easter when I was a kid, loved finding the chocolate our mom hid everywhere — inside pots and pans, set in the corners of the staircase leading to the basement, camouflaged in the plants, on the keys of our piano.

When I was little, I did a lot of pretending. Believed in the Easter Bunny and the Tooth Fairy long after my friends moved on from the myths. Mom and I read a lot of fairy tales together.

These days I wonder about the stories of Oz's Wicked Witch of the West, the Gingerbread House lady, Snow White's apple-bearing queen with her terrible mirror — what were their stories? How did they get so screwed up? I wonder if something bad happened to them, made them ugly.

DeNayer measures an eighteen-centimetre triangle, starting from the little hollow where my collarbones meet. We check it out, our three heads tilted to one side as we peer at the reflection of black dots he's made with a Jiffy marker. I think the dots don't match, the right one is a bit low. He measures again, says they match exactly — an optical illusion because the left scar is curved and the right one runs horizontally.

I say, "I'm not the best judge, go for it."

Back behind the curtains, the sterilized sheets in place, I feel the pinch of the freezing going in and laugh at their jokes about keeping the needle away from the implant. I watch the creation of my left nipple. I crane my neck forward, chin to chest and see De-Nayer mark a careful X with this purple pen. He takes the scalpel, moves it across the X and I feel its pressure, see him pick up a corner of my skin and pull it over to the other side and stitch it, take the opposite triangled piece of my skin and pull it across, stitch it, tie it. Dr. DeNayer explains to his resident how this special stitch creates the nipple, builds a tower of layers. He reminds me of an energetic cooking-show host explaining his fruit tray creations: pineapple-baskets and delicate apple-flowers, melon balls.

Needle in, needle out, pull tight. I remember stitching my daughter's Level 1 swimming badge onto her swimsuit. It took three tries — thread knotting, stitches too wide, too far away from the badge, thread coming out of the needle, pulling too tight, not pulling tight enough. I hope DeNayer is better at sewing than I am.

He tells me a story as he pulls, stitches, pulls, ties, about being a kid at his family's cottage and jumping, wrestling on the couch in wet bathing suits, how the upholstery wore away over the years; then as a med student home for the summer, mending the old couch with his curved needle. He finishes his story as he makes the final stitch on my right nipple; I can feel the double tug getting it tight, the resident leaning over me to cut the string, red now.

"They got a new couch," DeNayer says, "and you can't sit on it with wet bathing suits."

He starts on the left nipple, looks up at me over his mask, asks if I'm doing okay. I nod yes, keep going. The pattern on the ceiling panels looks like the scales of fish, or like rows and rows of nipples.

The resident is kind. Hand on my leg, patting my leg. Comfort, comfort. He has a wife, he says, young kids. I bet he's a good dad. I wonder if he'll tell his wife, when he comes home at the end of the day, that he gave some good old-fashioned TLC to some lady getting new nipples. He wipes my collarbone clean of the brown surgical disinfectant. DeNayer asks him about a man who must have been the patient before me; this is teaching time. The resident recounts the damage done by a 600-pound quad landing on the guy's face. His nose shattered. No doubt. How the splint created a scar in the shape of the letter L. How the wife said it was perfect: "L for Loser." DeNayer says next time use a Double-T-Bar splint. I laugh along with them — we three are having quite the good time, and the bizarre conversations taking place during something as serious as my reconstruction are just what I need.

I think about the work these doctors do, restoring the external after the internal is damaged. Shattered noses. Broken legs with protruding tibia bones. Burns. Breasts with cancer hollowed out of them and no nipples.

51

I wonder if they can fix my internal mess. There should be a tote for that in this place.

I close my eyes and think about my breasts. Too many times they were in the wrong place at the wrong time, and so they made me feel ugly. And they never nursed anyone and never will. Useless.

I used to wish I never had them. Then my wish was granted.

❦

"That's it, we're done." DeNayer and Gail smile down at me, the resident pats my leg again. I look up and then let my head fall back. Dr. Seuss would call them "Cat In The Hat" nipples, like a finger flopped on the end of what I have grown used to, my nice-looking new breasts. They are flesh coloured — no areola and as of yet un-tattooed. Just stitched on. Grotesque. I stare at the nipples on the textured ceiling, all in a row and nicely shaped. DeNayer says they will shrink as the breast pulls the nipple skin back into itself over the coming months. I knew this, he'd said so before we began that they would be huge at first. I put my shoes on, the hole in my sock now safe from sight. Gail hands me a brown paper bag filled with tape and gauze and tells me how to change my dressing. I close my eyes and imagine cutting gauze into 3x3 squares, taping them in layers on my breast, a Y-cut so my long nipples can lie safely protected. Flopping unless support-ed. Later, in a week or so, I'll be allowed to switch from gauze to the Dr. Scholl's corn removal bandages — their hollow circles a perfect fit.

I push through the "Out Patient Minor Surgery" doors. The man with the hoodie is gone, but the leftovers from his lunch are not — wet lettuce and pita crumbs in saran wrap remain on his chair. The three generations of thick Mennonite women watch me from their bench.

I stare back. Wonder what they're here to get fixed. Wonder if any of them are missing a breast or two. If in their world, they'd get new breasts or not.

I slip my hand inside my shirt, touch the raised scars running down across my chest, run my thumb across the bandages protecting these nipples-in-progress. Even if they are only symbolic, I need them. Reminders of loss, reminders that nursing new life can happen in lots of different ways.

"Mirror mirror on the wall, who is the fairest of them all?"

I can't stop crying. We are all the same. Fairy tale girl-heroes and hags. Even the witch knew she needed reconstruction. She just never booked the appointment. Minor surgery indeed.

"Always keep your tools in shape"

— from a carpenter's manual

Kate Braid

I ask my body now,
pump my breasts for information.
Does the skin tingle?
Is my joy aware of itself?
Is there a sort of exuberance
underneath it all, a foundation
of ebb and flow
and does the moontide sing in my veins?

Previously published in *Rough Ground Revisited* (Halfmoon Bay, BC: Caitlin Press, 2015)

CELEBRATE YOUR CURVES WITH FREE SHIPPING

Emily Wight

The thing about having big boobs, they say, is that everything is fine if you get fitted for a good bra. "A good bra" is never the bra you get off the sale rack at Victoria's Secret. "A good bra" is never twenty dollars. You are supposed to go to a real boutique where an older woman with soft hands fondles you and binds you with her measuring tape and recommends something in a letter size you didn't know existed for bras, and that costs over one hundred dollars. Probably more than that, if you don't want grandmotherly beige, and she will leave you to look at the black and lace bras and then you sneak away, ashamed because of money.

"Why not just buy it online?" they implore, those people who think you should get fitted for "a good bra" when you have lived your whole breasted life with "a good enough bra."

"Have you tried Amazon?"

Thirty-two is the number of years you have accumulated. Thirty-two is work and marriage and motherhood and trying not to let down whoever is watching. Thirty-two is still being alarmed at these responsibilities you're not sure you're mature enough to manage and all the bills that come with them. It is the endless march of time and suddenly you're aware that you are starting to feel things in your bones, like the weather and the fear of falling into traffic. You can't die in any kind of accident in this underwear, you think. You are both embarrassed of your big cotton underpants and alive in them, because they are devastatingly comfortable. Men get to be comfortable in their underpants, you think, so why can't you be too?

You can be comfortable, you just have to be careful.

You spend a long time looking at a Russet potato one evening while you are cooking dinner and see yourself in its lumps and its lopsided curvature. There you are. There. You don't sleep well because you worry yourself into a lather after dark, so you catch glimpses of infomercials from under a pile of knit blankets on the couch as you vacillate between REM sleep and panic. There's a better life out there, if you could just afford it.

You are a potato.

⟟⟟

You only notice the grease stains on your shirts when you get to work, when you're standing at the mirror under the aggressive fluorescent glow of the bathroom lights. The stains are always on your belly, which you can't see when you look straight down. That is where the food goes.

Though you are of average height, the world is not designed for you and so you stretch your long torso over countertops to reach objects, careful not to knock things over with your careless breasts. Your counters, full of foods half prepped and jars half spilled, are never as clean as you think or as you would like. You wear a lot of black, and a lot of acrylic sweaters which are not prone to staining.

At work, some of the women whisper about the Shopping Channel. Some women live by it, tracking sales and making purchases with interest-free payments over periods of months. They send you links and you scoff at them, because this is ridiculous. The Shopping Channel is ridiculous. And the links keep coming, in your email inbox and as text messages, because *LOOK! LOOK! LOOK!*

Yes, that ring is nice, you suppose. The shampoos and lotions seem expensive. Oh, you can buy a stand mixer? That's actually very affordable, at that price and with those payments. *Okay, I'll look. I'm looking.*

You don't know what channel the Shopping Channel is on, but the infomercials are on every channel after a certain hour. You have seen everything Dr. Ho has to offer, from decompression belts to digestive cleansing products. You have considered the Bowflex. You love the Magic Bullet infomercial because it is everything an infomercial should be, and even though you have a Magic Bullet and it is terrible, you still watch it every time it comes on, excited to see the lady smoking the fake cigarette and the dishevelled man with the apparent drinking problem and exaggerated hangover. You know more about infomercials than you know about real TV shows.

You don't know a lot of things about a lot of things other people seem to know about.

"Check Amazon. If you spend over twenty-five dollars you get free shipping."

Good enough is good enough is good enough.

The thing about having big boobs is that they don't age well, not like smaller boobs. Maybe if you had a decent bra they wouldn't give it all up to gravity. Maybe it would be more infuriating to spend two hundred dollars on a bra and still have saggy old-lady tits. Maybe we all end up with our boobs in our laps, in the end.

It is unreasonable to have to cart around more than a C-cup. It is uncomfortable, sweating under and between your D-plusses. They act like your boobs are sexual things but you have a hard time reconciling sexiness with the way your back hurts and the way your bra smells after the end of a long day.

You make it your private goal to ruin boobs for people who like them. Like telling people what's really in your food, you are a boob truther.

"I bet between her boobs smells a bit like cheese."

You are a rotten potato.

One day when you have had enough of your bra straps sliding down your shoulders, you relent and look at the Shopping Channel's website. There, they promise three Genie Bras for thirty dollars, which seems reasonable when you think of what a real bra would cost, and how little you spent on the one you're wearing for inconceivably less comfort.

Genie Bra: America's Top Selling Seamless Bras.

The whisper-soft fabric feels so fabulous against your skin, you'll even want to sleep in it.

Magic pouch accommodates removable modesty pads for extra lift and coverage.

You are going to do this. You are going to buy cheap, ugly comfortable bras. You think of your husband's hideous underwear, like bike shorts stamped with Costco's in-store brand, and the way he wears them until they have holes in them and no longer function as underwear and he's still wearing them. You think of your straps, slipping again and again and again, and how you don't really know what it means to wear supportive underthings. It is unreasonable to pay two hundred dollars for a bra. You couldn't if you wanted to, and if you could you certainly wouldn't. And it's not about not treating yourself. A two-hundred-dollar bra is only a treat for the person who gets to see it and you can't take it out at work, or show it off at dinner with your in-laws. What's the point? What's the point of anything?

You think of men not thinking this much about their underwear in their whole lives.

You take your credit card out of your purse and you type the numbers into the appropriate fields.

What is the point of anything, even.

CELEBRATE YOUR CURVES.

Good enough is better than you imagined, you realize, when your package of nylon-spandex bras finally arrives in the mail. Oh, they are hideous, like sports bras you'd buy at Walmart, but their engineering is sound and you think you must feel how other women feel with their smaller breasts or bras that cost more money.

Your husband doesn't have anything nice to say about your new bras so he doesn't say anything at all, and you shout at him for no reason but the actual reason is you have never known true comfort like this before and it is almost as if he has been denying you this by his unuttered expectation that your underwear impress him somehow.

He never said that.

You thought it, and now you are mad.

Now that you are comfortable, you should be careful or, at least, kind.

❧❧

You wonder if there are people who feel beautiful and comfortable at the same time.

You wonder if you are asking too much. Inner beauty is useless because people can't appreciate it from afar or be seduced by it if they are strangers or your husband after a fight.

Good enough is never really good enough. Your comfort runs counter to the expectations you perceive are there, upon you, even though no one's ever mentioned you specifically needing to get your sexy up.

It is hard to be a woman and have big breasts and to not know what to do with them.

It is hard to know how to be, even at thirty-two, which is how old you are now and the number of years you've spent not absorbing the critical details of womanhood and how to experience it flawlessly. And after spending twenty of those years in bras that never felt right, whose straps slid off your shoulders, you've found something that works for you and you can't even really enjoy it because of what it all might mean.

You are comfortable in your big underpants and your bra from the infomercials on late-night television.

You thought your body was the potato, but maybe your brain is.

What if you are the only one who thinks these things and then gets mad about them? You load the Shopping Channel website and click through to see what else on there might change your life.

"Free shipping on orders over twenty-five dollars," they say.

59

PINCHES

Taryn Hubbard

Grace had confidence. She took her speed bike down suicide hill. Flew past the field where the two horses lived. Barrelled across a major road without the slightest pressure on her brakes. The van she sliced past wasn't too happy, but whatever. It stopped.

"That's nasty," she said. About everything. Somehow even playing California kick-ball was nasty. This town we were stuck in was nasty. Sure, I knew that. Nasty, nasty!

Her hair was cropped short like Jean Seberg, but I didn't know the reference. She was taller than me, with freckles. Her bike was a junker from the 1980s. Those curly handlebars. Leaned in head first, no helmet. We sat together during class. It was grade six.

Her confidence radiated from the responsibility of wearing a real bra, I was sure of it. Not a trainer with stretch like the kind I wore. Authentic underwire. Polyester lace. Wearing a trainer meant I could forget to put it on and it wouldn't be a big deal, but a teen bra meant something tangible and threatening needed to be hidden. It meant maturity in all its confusing and isolating glory. I wasn't sure when it would happen for me, but maybe it would help with the bigger problems I had on my hands. Like the problem of Lyn. And the problem of just about all the other kids at school.

I know you're supposed to be relatively happy as a kid, but I was slowly losing any innocent sureness kids have. Grace was my friend because she was new and didn't know anyone, and I was her friend because all the other girls shunned me. And likewise me them. It was just harder for them to notice I was giving them a healthy dose of their own medicine because there were more of them, and the shunning spanned into the delinquent and tough grade sevens. An awkward sadness hung around me, so it was nice to have Grace to go on bike rides with after school.

Grace had been to ten different schools and was used to never fully finding her place in the order of the elementary school classroom. She had lived out and about Western Canada, mostly. Alberta. BC. A short stint in Ontario to live with her aunt. Her clothes were from thrift stores, but it suited her. She looked older than the rest of us, though it might have been her height and the sheer button-up grandma blouses she wore. This is how I knew she was wearing an adult bra.

It is not surprising to me that at age eleven I would think confidence came from finally getting boobs. Insecurities around bras and boobs consumed my media. It was the late 1990s and *Now and Then*, a film about a group of girls the same age as me dealing with a Hollywood portrayal of an idealized suburban adolescence, was supposed to reflect me and my (non-existent) friends. *Finally a movie about a group of girls*, said its producers. Teeny, played by Thora Birch, filled balloons and stuffed them into her bra to achieve a more mature and glamorous look, a boob hack perfected by filling her balloons with vanilla pudding instead of water. "Pudding has a heavier, more realistic texture," she told the other girls.

In *Now and Then*, the bond between females trumped everything, always. They were consistently there for each other, even as successful adults. Eventually Teeny got her boob job when she was an adult and became a Hollywood star, all the ingredients to make the perfect tabloid fodder. The movie was shit, yet I rented the VHS every chance I got.

The "group of best friends thing" did not resonate with me. I was more a one-on-one kind of friend. My kindred spirit friend moved away just before Grace arrived. We'd still send each other notes in the mail written on pink cartoon paper I bought at the Asian grocery store where she took me to get bubble tea. She didn't have boobs either, and it didn't matter because we were more interested in looking up local ghost stories at the library than hanging out with boys.

According to my mother, however, my boobs were huge. Much bigger than hers were at eleven. According to my grandmother and just about everyone else, boobs on preteens were a side effect of hormones in the chicken. As if our boobs had become GMOs themselves, drastically oversized and perky. Pairs of crisp apples, perfectly rounded mini watermelons. Or in my case, grape tomatoes. Seedless.

Grace made a great friend after school, but during school she didn't have the best attendance record. A stomach ache, fatigue, not doing her homework — something — kept her at home at least a few times a month. Every time she wasn't there, I had to face the girls who shunned me on my own.

Sometimes on the walk to school we'd meet up on the street because she lived close to me. On a not-so-atypical morning, she wasn't there, so I walked by myself. When I slipped through the gate, a group of girls who made it their mission in life to remind me how uncool I was were waiting for me. At the head of this pack was my former one-on-one best friend Lyn. The pack moved as a unit toward the school when the first bell rang, but Lyn hung back.

"LOSER!" she screamed. Everyone who was not in the building looked at me. Nobody looked at Lyn.

I shuddered, looked to the ground.

She ran back to her group and they laughed all the way to class.

❦

At night I read *Sweet Valley High*. Not only were the Wakefield sisters perfect and athletic size sixes, they also had the added benefit of being beautiful identical twins. Grace had an older sister, too. A mysterious woman who lived in the basement of the split-level house their mom rented. I never met her. At the time I thought she must be a full adult, but realistically she was likely in her teens. Grace and her sister fought.

"You're nasty," Grace yelled through the basement window. I was never invited inside her house and Grace was not available for sleepovers. We were friends, but more out of kindness to each other's situation (read: new kid and hated kid) than out of that rare connection people sometimes find in friendships. Grace, however,

62

also read *Sweet Valley High*, so we'd trade the books we had in the series.

Sweet Valley High felt edgier than the *Nancy Drew* series I'd been reading non-stop the summers before. It was also obviously trashy, which may have been why I liked it. Not about solving important mysteries, but more about Elizabeth keeping her vixen sister Jessica's wicked plots for high school domination in line.

If I made it to high school, I knew it would either be a continuation of the same stress from Lyn & Co. or something, hopefully, better.

❧❧

While *Now and Then* and *Sweet Valley High* were glimpses into a squeaky-clean teenagehood, the book *Are You There God? It's Me Margaret* was meant to explain everything. The awkwardness of not filling in (or fitting in), dealing with boys and making friendships. Judy Blume had the backstory I was waiting for. Margaret knew why life didn't make any sense and why growing up was difficult. My copy was passed down from my mother's preteen years, my aunt's name and address hand-printed in Bic ballpoint on the inside page. I was skeptical that this book would answer my questions, but I still read it.

Margaret is the new kid, still "flat" and praying for boobs, among other things. Learning all I know about religion from *The Simpsons*, I didn't feel God was a good resource to beg for a real bra, but still, I was mesmerized by Margaret. She was unsure of how this puberty thing was supposed to work out, but she was fearless anyway. A one-foot-in-front-of-the-other kind of girl.

We must, we must, we must increase our bust was the boob chant Margaret did with her friends, or maybe it was a self-esteem chant. The words were half pep-squad cheer and half "proto law of attraction, ask the universe and you shall receive" fluff. I tried it, just for fun, alone in my room. I doubt it worked.

Unlike *Sweet Valley High* and *Now and Then*, which I discussed with acquaintances at school, I didn't talk about what I was

63

learning about Margaret. It felt like secret research, like finally I was getting the inside scoop, and I didn't have confidence that anyone would understand me. The other girls probably didn't need this info. Lacking a sister, I always felt I was missing out on some important girl talk. I didn't even trade my copy with Grace. It was understood that this copy came from my grandma's house and couldn't be loaned out. I also knew my mom and her sisters read this book and survived, but it was still iffy territory that I couldn't share with anyone.

Margaret was amazing, even under pressure for not having breasts when everyone else was getting them. At her birthday, Freddy Barnett tried to give her a bit of luck: *Then he pinched me on the arm — really hard! Enough to make tears come to my eyes. He said, "That's a pinch to grow an inch. And you know where you need that inch!"* Her tears and Freddy's comfort in criticizing her body struck me. Unlike the characters in *Now and Then* and *Sweet Valley High*, who naturally filled in their role within society, Margaret knew expectations hurt. While Teeny filled her bra with vanilla pudding to capture the male gaze with her budding and voluptuous figure, Margaret stuck tiny cotton balls under her shirt. It was just enough to get by. Just enough to look like the other girls. To be normal enough to be invisible.

Grace was gone before the end of the school year. By then I had taken up martial arts, which added a new problem to my slowly blossoming chest. All of a sudden I had something on my body bounce when I did jumping jacks. Because of this, it was time I got a real bra. One I had to wear consistently. So off to Zellers I went with my mom. For one white bra.

I wish I could say that before Grace left we had a goodbye bike ride, but her mom moved the three of them quickly and I never heard where she moved to. I also wish I could say getting a bra allowed me to deal with my problems with Lyn like an adult, but I can't do that either. In fact, today she works as a dental assistant at my dental office and I pray every checkup that my usual assistant isn't away so I don't have her scaling my teeth. I can still imagine her muttering the word "loser" behind her hygiene mask. I have no idea where Grace ended up, and don't think I'll run into her again. Though I still wonder if she thinks everything is nasty.

A few years ago I found out the actress who played Chrissy DeWitt in *Now and Then* quit Hollywood and moved back to Canada sometime in her teens, taking up residence in the city about twenty minutes from me. A city I visited frequently because that's where my grandma lived. The actress died of an accidental heroin overdose at about the same age I am now, and it made me feel sad. I know it's no secret that child stars often have turbulent adulthoods, but it felt like a touch of that childhood innocence was gone. She was the motherly one in the movie, and the reason why they all come back together as adults. Their adulthood was imagined as one without social media, just phone calls and letters. Chrissy was the one who kept in touch.

Unlike actors in movies, I haven't had the same issue with finding out what happened to characters in books years after reading them. That's my imagination. Margaret is still that grade-six girl trying to figure it out, all while praying for boobs, and I like it that way.

First Class after Lunch — Mid-1960s

Marilyn Belak

Before all the bras were burned
they crossed our hearts
and butterfly tipped our breasts

pointed and separated
we sat
in grade ten chemistry

our eyes on the vapour
liquid nitrogen released
when Mr. Skinner froze
the wiener to demonstrate
state in Absolute Zero

and I intercepted
the note that read
"Marilyn is like a baseball,
all curves."

A Site of Potential

Nicole Boyce

I was eleven years old and obsessed with breasts. I was aware of breasts because I was aware of the Spice Girls, and Ginger Spice had breasts. I knew this because I had seen them perform magic: transforming a Union Jack into the shape of a female body. The other Spice Girls had breasts too, but it was Geri Halliwell's that were featured most prominently in the limited media of our household — the *Calgary Herald*, the Yahoo! homepage. It was her breasts that had been rumoured to have appeared unclothed, once, in the pages of a British magazine.

I was captivated by this concept: breasts. Breasts that could be covered and bare. Breasts that could be present, observing, the whole time a person was doing anything: auditioning for a band, performing on *Top of the Pops*. I pored over the Ginger Spice section of my Spice Girls book. There were Geri's breasts, in pictures of the band's early days. There they were on a teenage Geri with a blond bob, while she stretched out on some English lawn.

The Spice Girls' message was this: girls could do pretty much anything. Theirs was a media-palatable feminism, a mass-marketed call for female camaraderie. Platform shoes! Girl power! They chanted in *Spice World*: "We're the Spice Girls, yes indeed. Just Girl Power is all we need. We know how we got this far... strength and courage and a Wonderbra!"

I wanted a Wonderbra. More importantly, I wanted the breasts that could justify that Wonderbra. Not whatever was currently under my T-shirt, those tiny inklings that were too insubstantial to really understand, let alone grasp. I imagined grapefruits and softballs. I resented pancakes on principle. Breasts were my ambition.

The goal seemed, like many things at that age, just a matter of time. Though my mother is an A-cup and my older sister is an A-cup, and almost all the women on my mother's side of the family are A-cups, I eyed my paternal aunts jealously. They were my salvation, these short, Scottish women. I had seen them in bathing suits.

So I began to think of my chest as a site of potential, a work-in-progress. Always, there was the idea that something else was coming, chest-wise. That the *real* breasts — the physical envoys of that intriguing concept — hadn't yet arrived. I was sure if I focused hard enough on my lackluster buds, larger breasts would emerge from within, like some inverse version of a nesting doll.

By fifteen, I had breasts. Not the ones I'd wanted — dream D-cups had become definite A-cups — but something to hang my bra on. If we're being honest, one of them is probably a double-A, but it bolsters me to think of them as a matched set.

What I wanted now was not size, but access. I'd have accepted larger breasts in an instant, but I was more focused on the facts at hand. I had a boyfriend. He looked very handsome in his Korn hoodie. We had access to my parents' basement, and those seemed like the three ingredients for second base. I'd been plotting my arrival at this base since the Ginger Spice years, which had coincided with my understanding of the baseball metaphors in teen magazines. I would peer into *Seventeen*'s sealed sections at my local Chapters, studying eroticism but never completing the transaction.

I wasn't sure my boyfriend had an action plan for second base. We smushed ourselves together in school hallways, smearing spit on each other's chins, but our arms remained modest danglers. There was, briefly, the sense that my chest was hanging between us, an elephant much larger than its actual size. Second base felt inevitable, and that inevitability was awkward. I hoped he would eventually touch my breasts, and he hoped he would eventually touch my breasts, but neither of us knew how to approach it. If we could just get it together — his hands, my bra — I was sure it would unlock a whole new level of the sexual game. Eventually he did touch them, but it just unlocked hand jobs. We dated for a few months, and then my breasts and I were alone again, waiting for the next phase. I didn't think about it too deeply then, this waiting. But looking back, I do wonder: Why have I always related to my breasts this way? They've never just been what they were, in the moment — they were always about what they might become.

❦

At twenty-one, I found a lump. I came across it during a vicious hangover after one of those university parties that starts with a wish your life was more like *Felicity* and ends with a twisted ankle. When I woke up, my pillowcase smelled like Smirnoff Ice. I lay in bed doing a head-to-toe assessment of a body that felt like a 5'6" bruise. Yes, I still had ankles, not just throbbing chords of pain. Yes, I still had breasts. One of those breasts had a lump.

The lump was small, like a wad of gum someone had wedged in there. I could move it around, if I tried, and I did, tugging it this way and that, hoping I could smooth it with my fingers. I couldn't.

I kept thinking about *City Slickers*. There's this scene where each of the three main characters describes the best and worst day of his life. They're all riding on horses. Whimsical music swells in the background. After Billy Crystal's character, Mitch, describes a Yankees game with his dad, his friend asks about his worst day.

"Worst day?" Mitch says. "A couple years ago Barbara [his wife] finds a lump."

"What? Jesus."

"Yeah, it scared the shit out of me."

"You never said anything."

"Yeah, well, you know, it turned out to be nothing. But that whole day was…"

He looks down, not finishing the sentence. Even as a child, I remember intuiting the seriousness of this moment, the way it stood out from cattle-roping scenes and Ben & Jerry's jokes.

When it comes to breasts, mounds are what you're going for. Lumps can be dangerous.

I Googled:

"breast lump"

"breast lump, only twenty-one"

"breast lump, only twenty-one, no family history of cancer"

Message boards provided little comfort.

I went to my doctor. He's a meek, efficient man, who uses awkwardness as a sort of second glove, a natural barrier that prevents even the most tactful intimacy. By that time, I'd been his patient for two years, but he still treated my pap tests like a sort of vaginal hot potato, trying to jab in all the necessary instruments before some unknown timer dinged. I was at an age where many of my medical concerns were sexual: birth control prescriptions, STI testing, and now, this breast situation, and I pitied him, a little, for having to hear about my body so often.

"I found a lump," I choked out, heart pounding beneath my paper gown. I'd been unclothed in the room before, but had never felt vulnerable. My shaking voice embarrassed me.

The doctor touched my breast. Poked and prodded. I stared at posters for hepatitis vaccines, trying to ignore the troubled buzz of my thoughts.

"Yes," he finally said. "That's definitely a lump."

I started to cry.

"Why are you crying?" He looked genuinely puzzled.

Tears and snot. I didn't answer.

"Oh, are you — you're worried about *cancer?* Well..."

More tears, more snot.

"...it is a small possibility, but very rare in someone your age."

We sat quietly for the length of six snots, then he wrote me a requisition for a biopsy. I walked home. It was a forty-minute walk, but I saw no crosswalks, no cars. I looked at my feet and thought about death. At twenty-one, I still sometimes transposed the words morality and mortality, and hadn't given much serious thought to either. Though I'd had run-ins with nausea and minor scoliosis, I'd never been truly sick, and I'd just assumed, in my youthful, privileged way, that my body was like a soap opera: it wouldn't run forever, but it wasn't stopping anytime soon.

And now, this lump. How would I tell my mother? I'd always assumed my breasts would grow, but it never occurred to me that their growth could be dangerous. How ridiculous, that such a tiny part of me could hide something so critical. Suddenly my body seemed secretive. It had a thousand drawers to hide things in.

For the next three weeks, I sleepwalked through my social life. I zoned out during shifts at the discount shoe store. In the evenings, I thought about death. I listened to goth songs — grim leftovers from my adolescence — and thought of all the things I'd wanted, and still wanted, and had assumed that time would deliver to me. When I wasn't thinking about death, the strangest, most contraband thoughts flashed through my mind, thoughts that surprised and ashamed me. Lying on an ultrasound table, cold gel against my skin, I found myself thinking: I can finally get a boob job. After the surgery, if there is an after. I'll get C-cups after all.

The lump, it turned out, was benign. It was a fibroadenoma: a non-cancerous tumour made up of glandular tissue. The day I got the results, I sat on my hardwood floor in pajama pants, unwriting the scenarios I'd been fleshing out all month. There would be no surgical gurneys wheeled down ominous hallways (an image I'd borrowed from *Grey's Anatomy*). There would be no saucy wigs or stylish headscarves (a wardrobe prospect I'd borrowed from *Sex and the City*). The internet told me fibroadenomas were sometimes called "breast mice" because they can move around within tissue. A breast mouse, then: small and harmless.

It's now been nine years since my biopsy — no trace of the procedure left but a sprinkle-sized scar. Sometimes I still think about the way the older women looked at me in the diagnostic centre — all of us wrapped in navy smocks — as if I'd learned something too early. When really, I'd just glimpsed another scene of potential: a version of my life undestined to become reality.

Maybe that's what I really wait for — the broadening of perspective each new scenario brings. Breasts lend themselves well to speculation: they are my access point for envisioning the future.

With the lump scare behind me, it's sometimes tempting to consider my breasts finished, to make peace with their current iteration and call it a day. There's this desire to accept my breasts in the now (Carpe diem! Seize your A-cups!). But I can't help thinking — even as I'm envisioning this pleasant stasis — about other possibilities on the horizon. Motherhood. Milk. A utilitarian functionality that's been dormant all along. My friends tell me about nursing pads and nipple shields, the potential equipment of my breasts' next stage. There is always new terminology to explore, new ways to become, once again, curious about my body. And perhaps it's this waiting I must really learn to accept, rather than the breasts themselves. To embrace my speculations as a flexible means of acceptance — the way I've chosen to understand these unfinished A-cups, whatever uncertainties our future may hold.

Pep Talk

Zuri Scrivens

"Do you want to touch them?"

I wait, smiling patiently while her eyes scan the room to make sure no one is watching. Music pulses out from a stereo behind the bar, and a few of our teammates playfully toss each other around the dance floor. The seasoned veterans are immersed in their drinks at tables scattered throughout the clubhouse, reminiscing about the day's victory against our rival team. No one is the wiser. Rachel has only been playing rugby with us for a little over a month, but she takes my question in stride. For all she knows, this is part of being a rookie, and the wrong answer could seriously jeopardize her reputation on the team. Fortunately for her, though, this is just how I break the ice — exposing the elephant in the room for all of its attempts to remain ashamed and invisible. There is nothing to be ashamed of here.

I can see that she doesn't know if she can trust me — it's not every day that your teammate asks you to feel her breasts.

"Yes?" It's more of a question, but I'll take it. I grab her hand and place it on my right side, just below my armpit and over the long, curved scar.

"See? Rock hard, right?"

Rachel's eyes bulge back at me, and I move her hand slowly across an identical scar line on my left breast. Her mouth drops open as her fingers pass the lumps and edges of a metal sphere lying beneath it.

"That's where they inject it. The saline. That's how they expand my chest slowly — like a water balloon."

"Seriously?"

I nod and let go while she continues to feel around my breasts, searching for the nipples that are no longer there. In this moment, any bitterness or sadness I have felt is gone, yielding to the strange, innate part of me that finds cancer fascinating. My dad has been a surgeon since the 1960s, and it has always been a secret pleasure of mine to eavesdrop on his conversations with his colleagues. I study the words he uses — a different language entirely. Aneurysm. Varicose veins. Balloon angioplasty. Claudication. Peritoneum. The Latin rolls off his tongue in his thick, hybrid Canadian-Grenadian accent. Over time I've learned what they all refer to. What is a test, and what is a disease. What is thoracic, and what is vascular.

What is cancer.

What is fatal.

I watch Rachel carefully, making sure that she isn't somehow getting off on this, that it's strictly an educational experience. In a way, I see this as my duty to society — one small way to make cancer less frightening to the population as a whole. To take away its power. Besides, I can't feel anything across the area that was once my boobs. Only a bit of pressure to indicate that something is touching me. The old sensations are permanently gone.

❧❧

I vividly remember the sensation of feeding my son from my breasts. As a new mother, I struggled to master the art of nursing, and the first two weeks of Michael's life were spent in agonizing frustration. I couldn't understand how something that was supposed to be so natural could be so challenging. I had heard so many stories of women who had brought their newborn babies to their breast right after birth, only to have them immediately latch on and begin to suckle; but that was not my story. It took two weeks of only being able to stand while nursing — an odd trick that somehow worked for us — but eventually Michael and I had it figured out. Soon, it became an experience that I cherished. I enjoyed the firmness of his infant mouth around my nipples — frenzied, yet somehow calming — and the relief that it gave my breasts as they emptied. His rhythmic sucking was pleasurable without being sexual in any way. The sense of a

74

primordial connection was there, and I relished the moments that followed each feed. Michael would inevitably lapse into a peaceful milk coma, me gazing at his tiny mouth, slightly open and curled into a smile. It was a give-and-take relationship. I planned to maintain it for as long as possible but ten short months later that plan was shattered.

When I first found it, I assumed that the large lump in my right breast was a clogged milk duct and tried to deal with it on my own. I figured it was something every nursing mother experienced. After a week of lying around the house with refrigerated cabbage leaves across my chest — an old wives' tale for reducing breast inflammation — I noticed a swollen lymph node in my armpit on the same side. I ditched the cabbage leaves and made an appointment with my family doctor. Dr. Carter put me on antibiotics, a fruitless attempt at shrinking my offending lump. I think a small part of me knew. Normally a diligent pill taker, I didn't even bother to complete the entire course of antibiotics this time, and when I went back to see the doctor, the lump and the swollen gland were still there — unchanged.

Later that week, I walked through the haze of smoke towards the doors of Royal Columbian Hospital, the parking lot bordered with patients on one side. Patients in yellow and blue gowns, sitting in wheelchairs, faces wrinkled and gaunt. Cigarettes dangling from mouths that savoured every last breath drawn on the very thing that brought them to that place. I made an exaggerated show of holding my breath, making pointed glances at the fluorescent yellow "No Smoking" signs. I carried on through the doors, following the red arrows, leading me like Hansel and Gretel. I had been through my fair share of ultrasounds the year before; my pregnancy hadn't been easy. Three stubborn uterine fibroids grew to the size of golf balls and made what was supposed to be a glowing milestone in my life a complete nightmare. After two separate hospital stays, one day visit, monthly ultrasounds and a scheduled C-section, I had become a seasoned pro at subjecting myself to medical tests. I wasn't concerned about getting through this one at all. However, when the technician cleaned the slick conductive gel from my breast and told me to go directly from ultrasound to the mammography waiting room, a surprised chill ran through my body.

Mammograms are for those other women. Older women. Women in their forties and fifties and sixties. Women who have had their babies and have watched their babies grow up into graduates, then parents themselves. Women with hair more grey than brown. Women of wisdom. Women who maybe know a thing or two about handling life's challenges. Mammograms are not for those of us just entering their thirties. They are not for those of us with newborns. Nothing about being in that place made sense to me. I was only thirty-three years old, yet heading towards having my breast sandwiched between two cold metal plates.

I wrapped the blue hospital gown tight around my waist, taking in the two other women in the waiting room. I tried to catch their eyes. Tried to seek out their confidence. Their courage. Instead, a complete breakdown was just on the other side of those eyes. In their faces I saw every woman I had ever looked up to but never found a way to relate to. Now, there was nothing to divide us.

I skimmed through the pages of an old *Canadian Living* magazine as each woman was called away by a technician. Not much older than me, the tech was an athletic-looking brunette with a seasoned poker face — kindness and empathy, but nothing telling.

"Zuri Scrivens?" I didn't want to answer. Some strange part of me wondered if someone might recognize my name. Of all the feelings I could have felt, embarrassment had been the least expected. Cringing at the sound of my own name, I looked up from the magazine.

"Zuri?" The technician offered a quick smile. "It's just this way."

The mammography room was cold and a bit larger than I expected. A counter with shelves lined one side of the room, while a computer screen and chair sat perched behind a small, standalone window — presumably to protect the technician from the x-rays which I was about to be hit with. Just a few feet from the computer stood a machine with two large metal plates, so reminiscent of getting my eyes checked that I nearly moved to place my chin on the plates in front of me. Instead, I opened my gown at the top and placed my right breast between the two waiting plates.

"Okay, now. Grab these two bars on either side of you with your hands and stay as still as you possibly can. Don't move a muscle. Don't even breathe. Great. Okay, I'll be right back. Remember, try not to move."

I'm not one for cold showers, nor the Polar Bear Swim, so it's safe to say that my breasts had never touched something quite so cold. Yet, after a few seconds, it was almost soothing — that is, until the upper plate began to firmly squeeze down on my breast. I winced, then told myself to relax, that it wasn't so bad. When the squeezing ended and images had been taken of both sides, I thought my breasts might retain their flattened shape. Instead they just dropped back to their usual low-lying position, easily re-inflating with milk, tissues and air.

"Okay, Zuri, please get changed then wait back in the waiting room."

I was surprised that she wanted me to stay. I thought I was done, that the test would finish and I could just walk away. Suddenly I was more concerned than I had been up to that point. It's never a good sign when they make you wait.

I stole away to one of the empty changing stalls to remove the gown and get back into my clothes. The waiting room was eerily silent. It felt like an eternity of "This Summer's Best Meal Plans" and "July Beauty Tips," but I'm sure it was only minutes of skimming the *Canadian Living* magazine before the technician came back to find me.

"Zuri, we'd like to book you in for a biopsy later this week. Can you come in again?" Her poker face was starting to fade.

"Um, sure. Yes, of course." My words came thick and cautious. She wanted to biopsy the mass and conduct a fine needle aspiration of the lymph node. All I wanted was to run from that hospital and never return.

When I did come back the following week, the women in the waiting room were different, but their eyes were still the same. Sad. Overwhelmed. Afraid. Eyes that reflected mine. We all needed a pep talk — something to give us a shot of courage. I wanted to march around that room and give them all fist bumps. I wanted to look them in their eyes, tell them that we've got this. Whatever "this" is — we've got it. To no longer be afraid.

The technician called me into the ultrasound room. My fears faded momentarily as we learned that we had two mutual friends — a couple whom we both admired deeply. Chatting about our friends was enough to distract me such that I didn't notice her poker face, or whether she even had one. When I left, I had no sense of what my results might be; I even felt somewhat excited. Our conversation left me feeling lighthearted and somehow I took this to mean that everything was okay.

Three days later, I sat in Dr. Carter's office waiting for the good news. She didn't waste any time — only enough to clear her voice and face of any and all feelings.

"I'm afraid it's cancer."

The air was thick with her words, and I began to choke it all down. I wanted to smack her as she sat nodding her head with pursed lips — as if somehow, I had screwed this up. I don't remember anything Dr. Carter said after those shocking words; but I do know that I didn't shed a single tear in that cold medical room.

As I drove home, the radio blasting and tears streaming down my face, Pat Benatar belted out her defiant song "Hit Me With Your Best Shot," insisting that I had what it took to conquer the news I had just been given. From that moment, failure was never an option.

Five years, three surgeries, twelve rounds of chemotherapy, two shaved heads and one course of radiation later, I spend every morning staring at the woman/man/boy-girl-child staring back

at me through the bathroom mirror. I don't know this androgynous being. Every day I lay my hand where my breasts should
be. Where nipples used to be. Dollar-sized metal circles lay just
beneath the skin at the centre of each "breast," beacons for filling
up. Once for mother's milk, now for saline. Salt and water in a
bag beneath my chest. Sixty cc's poked through my metal mag-
netic nipple. Growing. Growing. Enough. It was too much the
last two times. Squeezed between my pectoralis muscles and my
ribs, the tissue expanders felt as if they were pushing my entire rib
cage through my back. The pain from the increased pressure was
unbearable; and even though it was quickly remedied by some
leftover Tylenol 3s, I was done. I had never craved big breasts.
I loved sports, especially aggressive sports, and I always saw my
breasts as more of a hindrance than anything. By the time I hit my
twenties and began playing rugby, I wished that I had a flat chest.
I remember discreetly comparing my breasts to those of my less
endowed teammates in the change rooms, and I'd secretly envy
their luck. I don't think my plastic surgeon believed me when I
first told him that I'd prefer to go no higher than an A-cup. The
smaller the better, I told him.

❧

As it turns out, my chest wall was so damaged by the radiation
that an A-cup was all my body would allow. Tissue expanders do
just what they say, slowly expanding a woman's chest wall and
stretching her skin to create a space for her implants later on.
Unless you've had a significantly swollen body part at some point
in your life, it can be difficult to imagine what this might feel like.
I liken it to the type of pressure you feel on a balloon as you blow
it up. Hard and taut.

Even though I had once wanted A-cups, I did not want cancer
— let alone to have my breasts removed completely. I became surprisingly attached to nursing, and even now — modelling positivity
for my bewildered rugby teammate — it breaks my heart that I
will never nurse a child again. But I try not to dwell too much on

the sacrifice, and what I have lost. Instead, I think of the time I've gained to spend with my son, my husband, my family and friends. Instead I talk. I listen. I answer questions — and I let random people feel my boobs.

I watch Rachel's eyes lower as she lets her hand fall away from what has become of my chest. I can see that she is sad. Overwhelmed. Afraid. I think about what it's like to wake up and gaze at my naked body every morning. As important as it has been for me to understand and accept, I want others to understand too. I don't want her to feel sad for me. I am here. I am alive.

I smile, taking her hand and closing it into a fist, firmly bringing mine up to hers.

"Hey," I say to her. She looks at me, her eyes perking up a bit. "I'll have a fresh set of boobs by the time I hit my forties — how many women can say that?"

She grins and bumps my fist.

KNOBS

Jane Eaton Hamilton

we sold corn from a card table at the end of the driveway,
and men snapped out of cars like rewinding measuring tapes in
ties wrenched from their necks top buttons undone sweat stains
under armpits
　i refused to wear a shirt because my brother didn't have to
　you sure you want to show off your knobs, girly?
　i looked down at my knobs, across at my brother's knobs
　you been at church honey? this is the lord's day not a day for
ruination
　one man revved away but another squealed in to take his place
　long appreciative wolf whistle
　exhibiting your titties today? give you a dime to turn around
and pull down your shorts for me
　do you want corn?
　new man roared in, sweat on his forehead
　what you sellin', honey? sure it's corn on the cob?
　i looked down at tassels ejecting from the ears i said how
many you want mister?
　he said i want to shuck every last one hard and fast his tongue
came out pink and thick
　looked like he needed a salt lick
　i said 25 cents
　green leaves and corn silk
　dark yellow niblets
　he flicked my nipple
　he said i will give you 50 cents if you come over here and sit
in my car
　my brother said 25 cents voice hollow mister take them all
you can have them we don't want them
　corn gone, turquoise fins waving blue plumes laying rubber

Boobs

you only get 5 cents said my brother cause you're a girl
i get half i said 12.5 cents
nu-uh
i said do so thinking of wagon wheels I could buy
he said put on a shirt

THE PENCIL TEST

Christina Myers

The first time I heard about the pencil test, I was sitting in a sea of sleeping bags and pillows, giddy on a combination of 7-Up and gossip. I was twelve and midway through one of my first big sleepover parties. Our host, the queen bee of our little hive, held up a pencil and explained the process.

"You put the pencil right under your boobs, like this," she said, pressing it close to her tank-top-covered rib cage, just under the swell of her small breasts. "Then you let go. If the pencil stays there, you have... *saggy... boobs.*"

She let that sink in as we groaned and giggled, then released the pencil. It fell to the ground, no saggy boob in sight to trap it. She grinned. "If it falls, you're okay."

Sleepovers are like bootcamp for girlhood, endless hours of talking about boys and kissing, painting toenails and pretending to be older than you really are. We'd already played Truth or Dare, made a prank phone call or two. We'd sat mesmerized, watching the newly released *Dirty Dancing* — the VHS tape and machine both rented specially for the evening — then hashed over the plot, the characters, the clothes, the hair.

Just as we were beginning to settle down to sleep, Rosie — the birthday girl, whose mother was cool enough to rent *Dirty Dancing* and let us drink as many 7-Ups as we wanted — had stood up to tell us about the pencil test.

It didn't occur to me to wonder where she'd gotten this information. She said it so authoritatively — one hip cocked to the side, eyebrow arched, confident grin — that it brooked no debate among our gaggle of girls.

I giggled and "ewww gross"-ed along with the others, feigning mortification over the horror of imperfect breasts, all while hunching deeply into my Garfield nightshirt, keeping my own

83

chest — certainly the biggest in the room — hidden as well as I could manage. "Your turn," she said, bending over to retrieve the pencil and handing it off to the girl nearest her.

That's when my panic set in. The pencil test wasn't something we were just going to talk about, it was something we were going to do. In front of each other. Doing what we girls do best at thirteen — sizing up, ranking, judging, not so much to find fault in others but to figure out how much fault belongs to us.

❦

A year earlier, I'd woken up early on a spring morning to get ready for a family wedding and discovered that, sometime overnight, the "blossoming womanhood" fairy had arrived in a crampy, uncomfortable, confusing manner. Not nearly as exciting as the tooth fairy, let me assure you, and instead of cash gifts, I was left with a box of Kotex pads — each of which looked to me about the size and thickness of the Danielle Steel novels I wasn't supposed to read.

The arrival of my period — the first among my group of friends — was the harbinger of other changes, most notably that my mother finally decided it was far past the time for me to start wearing a support garment of some variety.

❦

We think of airplanes passing overhead as loud. Chainsaws, too, or cars backfiring or the sudden thunder of a summer rainstorm. None of these match, in volume, the sound of your own mother's voice in the Sears lingerie department asking the clerk for assistance to FIND A BRA FOR MY DAUGHTER!

My mother is actually a wonderfully supportive type, and certainly not the kind to be dismissive over pubescent mortification, but in that moment, her mild-mannered approach felt and sounded like the loudest and most public admission of unwanted cleavage in the history of the world. I was so horrified by the

84

entire proceedings that I've blocked the rest of the memory completely. I know this much: it was white, and there was a tiny pink
rosebud between the cups, and when I got home it went directly
into my drawer, where it stayed for a very long time.

In the logic of childhood, if it didn't exist, neither did my boobs.
In truth, I needed that bra. My breasts weren't just starting to grow,
they were already there. I hid them under big shirts, layers of sweaters with snug tank tops underneath, and learned to sit, walk, read,
breathe and live slightly curved over, to minimize their appearance.

I didn't know anyone else who had a box of Kotex in her
backpack, or a white bra in her drawer. I refused to be the first.

By the time I was old enough to be sitting in that sea of sleeping
bags and pillows at a sleepover with a racy movie, *having* breasts
wasn't really that big of a deal anymore. Most girls had them, or
at least the start of them — and of course, retrospectively I realize
that the torture I felt over my big ones was the parallel torture of
the girls who worried over their small ones. But just then, as we
sat in that circle, and the pencil was being handed off to the next
victim, I had no sympathy for the breastless. No, I envied them.
I wanted to be them: lithe, and slim, with bodies like Romanian
gymnasts who made perfect 10s at the Olympics. When the pencil
made its way around to them, they wouldn't need to fear whether
it would fall to their feet or stay trapped.

As Rosie held the pencil out to that first girl, and my heart
thudded in my ears and my face burned red, I knew with total
sinking certainty that I would fail the pencil test.

Are there any girls that came of age in the '80s who didn't want
to be Baby in *Dirty Dancing*? She was smart and funny, traits we
still believed were important, traits we hadn't yet given up as being "dorky" or "unattractive." She was awkward and nervous, she

didn't know how to kiss or dance or even how to do her hair properly or match her shoes to her dress. She was us, basically.

And Johnny. We might not have completely understood what sex was just yet, but we knew Johnny was, somehow, sex — at least in a safe, soft sort of way. He was world-weary but kind, gentle but passionate, and Patrick Swayze was just so goddamn good-looking that you wanted to die. We all wanted him. More importantly, we wanted to be what he wanted: the girl who shows up in Keds, carrying a watermelon, a tangle of clumsy uncertainty, and unfolds like a flower into a desirable woman for whom you'd fight society just to *dance* with.

Even as I wished for it, I knew: I was no Baby.

Baby would have passed that pencil test with flying colours.

Her huge-breasted sister, on the other hand, had a chest that practically entered the room before she did. When she was made foolish and silly and ridiculous in all her bouncing and breastiness, when she was manhandled and mistreated, I don't think we felt any sympathy for her. What did someone expect, looking like that?

❧

I managed to escape the pencil test that night. Thank god for the short attention spans of teenaged girls high on 7-Up and gossip. We moved on to something else, someone else, a new game or another story.

But I left that party with that pencil in my head and it stayed there for thirty-some-odd years. As I got older, I made jokes about the pencil test, cackling over the various objects I might keep under there. A pencil? Heck, why not the whole pencil case? How about a notebook? Box of Kleenex?

I laughed because it was easier than admitting that every single time I took my shirt off, every single time I tried on a bra, every single time a man saw me naked or I saw myself naked or I got undressed at the doctor's office, I thought of that rec room and that sea of pillows and that pencil and the sinking, horrible feeling that I was not Baby, and Baby was not me.

86

And then, one day, as I wove through traffic, half-heartedly listening to CBC Radio, I heard the words "pencil test." I turned up the volume, but I was too late, catching only the tail end of a discussion about women's bodies and self-image. When I got home, I Googled pencil test — breath held, anxious to see that my childhood ghost indeed had a place in reality.

From Wikipedia: "A pencil is placed in the infra-mammary fold, between the breast and chest. If the pencil does not fall, the woman has 'failed the pencil test' and needs to wear a bra."

What? The woman needs to wear a bra? Not "the woman has awful breasts" or "the woman has failed in growing boobs that defy the laws of physics in their perkiness" but "needs to wear a bra"?

The pencil test, it turned out, had been devised by Ann Landers as a simple — though tacky — measure of whether or not a young woman should *start* wearing a bra.

I followed the links at the end of the Wikipedia entry and found more, in particular, this: "if the pencil stays put, then she is officially a woman, with all the attendant glories."

I wanted to cry, for not having realized years ago that womanhood even *came* with attendant glories, that breasts that could keep a pencil in place were no better or worse than those that could not, that the test had been explained backwards or that it existed at all. It was too late to go back and re-do the first time I got to third base and hesitated — that damn pencil in my head; it was too late to go back and buy the pretty bras instead of punishing myself with the simple ones; it was too late to not wear turtlenecks for the majority of my twenties and thirties; it was too late to not apologize to the mammogram technician because she had to deal with my imperfect breasts.

How had I let something so foolish and insignificant define me for so long, so deeply?

Somewhere inside me, my twelve-year-old self, huddled in a Garfield nightie, desperate to escape that rec room, finally stood up, grabbed the pencil and cracked it in half.

A-T-C-G — All the Cancer Grief

Annie Parker

It was my last night in Lakeridge Health Hospital, four days after the doctors had removed my left breast. I tried to sleep, but couldn't. It was impossible to get comfortable. I was incredibly anxious about going home, where I knew I would have to face the repercussions of my mastectomy. I was overwhelmed. I thought about asking the nurse for a sleeping pill, but decided against it. I knew a pill would knock me out and that meant I wouldn't be able to do what I needed to do.

I looked toward the bathroom door. It was barely ajar and a sliver of light shone from inside. As a young girl, I had gotten into the habit of leaving the bathroom door open a crack with the light on, in case I had to get up in the middle of the night.

I slowly slipped my feet into my slippers and held my gown close to my body. I staggered just a little as I made my way toward the bathroom door. Once again, horrible sensations took over my body; I felt severe pounding in my heart and a loud thumping in my ears. I wanted to scream: MAKE IT STOP!

Reaching the bathroom, I had to sit down on the toilet seat. I felt utterly broken, empty and completely alone. Anne, I told myself, you need to build up a fortress inside for that little girl in you who needs others to get through life.

There, alone in that small hospital bathroom, I had no one to lean on. I was about to confront the physical truth of what had happened to me. I had to do this on my own. At that moment, in the small hospital bathroom, I came to grips with my new reality. I stood in front of the mirror and looked at my reflection. I hadn't showered in days because of the tube and bandages. I looked so white, ghost-like, my skin drained of colour, and my dark hair hung in clumps around my face. I spoke aloud, "Damn, girl, you look a little bit scary." Even with myself, I was trying to disguise my apprehension with humour but knew I was only delaying the inevitable: "Come on, Anne. You can do this."

With one movement, I dropped my hospital gown down to expose what would be my everyday appearance for the rest of my life. The shock of what I saw silenced the scream that rose up in me. Then I filled that silence with sobs: I cried and I cried and I cried. I looked like a freak. My entire left breast, complete with my nipple, was gone. My chest was weirdly concave. What remained were countless stitches — I lost track at thirty. There was dried blood from my left armpit to my right breast. The purple bruising was extensive. I kept saying over and over again, "I need to take a shower. I need to take a shower."

I reached for the string on the wall labelled "Nurse," pulled it hard and didn't let go. When the nurse arrived I could tell by the sympathetic look on her face that she knew exactly what I had just observed.

"Please, I need to take a shower," I begged her.

"It's late," she said. "Can you possibly wait until morning?"

"NO!" I snapped. "I need to clean myself up." Now it was anger instead of humour to disguise my devastation and to camouflage my tears.

The nurse was very kind. She helped me clean my body and get rid of the blood and antiseptic wash that had been applied before surgery. The orangey-brown liquid was used to help prevent infection but I wanted to wash away any evidence of the operation. I felt so dirty and violated. When the nurse tucked me back into bed, I was physically exhausted, mentally drained. The weak dawn light touched the face of the clock that I had watched almost constantly since sunset the night before.

June 25, 1980. I was on my way home. I was in quite a bit of pain, and there was a tightness and tingling where my left breast used to be. I had difficulty moving my left arm and shoulder; both were weak and heavy. But none of that mattered in the least when I crossed over the threshold of my front door and arrived straight into the arms of my son, Tyler.

In the weeks that followed, there was an obvious strain between Ron and me. Nothing I did or said could lighten the tension between us. Day after day, we grew further and further apart. Ron was distancing himself and I had no idea what to do. Had my obsession with cancer and my health interfered with what Ron needed? I remembered my father and how he had completely relied on my mother for emotional support. Maybe it was as simple as that. Maybe Ron didn't feel emotionally supported. Then I thought: What about my need for emotional support? I couldn't dwell on these worries about Ron and our relationship; just trying to cope with the physical aftermath of my surgery was difficult enough for me. I couldn't deal with anything else right then.

During this time, I isolated myself from my friends, my family and from Ron. I delved further and deeper into the research into cancer. Somewhere, somehow, I had to find a genetic connection. I educated myself on the essentials of human biology in hope that it might somehow shed an ounce of insight. It was the only thing I could think of that would explain what nature had done to my family. As with any devastating life event, I needed to understand why. I had so many questions that needed answering.

Life's twists and turns, I thought, are just like DNA's double helix, as explained in the medical encyclopedias I scoured for information. I read that DNA (deoxyribonucleic acid) encodes genetic instruction; this convinced me that my genetic instruction had predetermined cancer. I tried to understand how the double helix could coil in perfection yet be defective. I needed to find proof that my DNA contained a mutant cell, one that had caused my life to spiral out of control.

I continued to ask the questions I had always asked: Why me? Why Joanie? Why my mother? How many other women had experienced the same emotional hell I was going through? How many families believed hereditary cancer existed because of their own experience with the disease? How many children had lost their mother because of this? How many girls would turn sixteen, graduate from high school, marry and have children without a mother to guide them? How many young boys would watch as their mother was buried in the ground? Would they have support to help them through the anguish? My obsession intensified. If there were any other families in the world like mine, I wanted to help them as well.

It seemed an impossible task. I looked at my medical encyclopedias once again. I thought about the four nitrogen bases of DNA I had studied: adenine, thymine, cytosine and guanine; often referred to by their first letters, A-T-C-G. In my mind those letters stood for other words regarding my genetic makeup.

A-T-C-G. All The Cancer Grief.

I set my books aside and remembered my mother and my sister. I wished Joanie were here. I needed her. I thought about Joanie's — my — pearl necklace. I got up, went to my bedroom and found my jewellery box. I took out the necklace and put it on. I looked in the mirror. The pearls shimmered with loveliness; they were exquisite and deserved to be admired. For the first time in a while, I smiled. I decided to make a special dinner for Ron. Wearing the pearl necklace not only made me feel connected to the two women I loved the most, it also made me want to be attractive to the one man I loved the most. It made me want Ron to touch me the way he used to. It was only about six weeks after my operation, but I was desperate for life to return to normal.

I decided I would make his favourite meal, wear his favourite dress, and walk his favourite walk. I was determined that I would be sexy again and he would want me again. I prepared shrimp cocktails, roasted Cornish game hens and baked a cheesecake for dessert. It got later and later, and still Ron did not come home. I felt like the necklace around my neck: beautiful, but delicate and vulnerable. Only a mere strand of silk held the pearls together. Like the pearls, I felt as if my own life was hanging by a thread. Trying to discover the truth of a hereditary flaw in the genetic code, struggling to make sense of my life, was leading me through a twisted mess that I was unable to figure out or confirm.

I decided to be optimistic. I set the table with sparkling silver and our best wedding china, gold-edged and white, with an elegant, lacy green border. I set the arrangement of pink and purple flowers I'd bought that afternoon from the florist in the centre of the linen-covered table. It was a small attempt to place a burst of colour back into our lifeless relationship. I stood back and leaned against the kitchen counter. I gazed at the table, where the trailing greenery of the floral centrepiece looked beautiful among the shining tableware. I was sure that Ron would notice the hard work I had put into making the evening special. He had to. I needed him to recognize my sincerity and appreciate the gesture.

I was so relieved when I heard the front door open. I took a seat at the table. I was so anxious that the evening be a success, I shifted about, trying to strike just the right pose — sophisticated but also sexy.

Ron came into the dining room and looked around. He raised his eyebrows and wrinkled his nose. "What's all this?" he asked.

"I made it specially for you, for us," I said.

Ron turned away. "I already have plans."

"Wait! Please!"

Ron grunted as he exhaled, turning back around. "What? What do you want?"

"I thought we could, you know, spend some time together, have a quiet dinner, relax, and then maybe, you know…" I took my index finger and curled it around the pearls of my necklace. I lifted the necklace and ran the back of my fingers up my neck seductively.

Ron sneered, "What are you doing?"

I was embarrassed. I slapped my hand down on the table and stood up. "I want us to talk about what is happening to our relationship."

Ron laughed an empty laugh. The look on his face seemed to say, "Well, I don't." We stood in complete silence for a moment. I then sat back down at the table and filled my plate. Ron finally took a seat and did the same.

We began to eat, but neither of us spoke. I wasn't going to break the silence until Ron looked at me. Finally, he glanced my way, so I said, "It's important to me that you look at my scar. I need you to understand that breasts are only a part of what makes up a woman, and not really the most important part." Ron tossed his fork on the plate and, once again, exhaled in frustration. I knew dinner was over.

I slowly began to unbutton my blouse. "Please," I said. "Please look at me. Please touch me."

Ron rebutted, "I do touch you."

"I don't mean from the waist down. I want you to see my scar."

Ron threw his napkin on the table and stood up.

"Where are you going?" I asked.

"I'm going out." He turned to leave.

In desperation I bolted out of my chair and ran over to Ron. I grabbed his arm, pulled him round and forced him to face me.

"I am not letting you leave until you look at my scar!"

Ron grabbed at me in anger. I knew things were getting out of hand but I didn't care. I screamed at him, "Why won't you talk to me about what's wrong?"

He screamed back, "You're crazy!"

I became frantic. He has to see this, I thought. If only he would just look at my scar he might understand and our marriage could get back on track. I continued to undo my buttons and remove my blouse.

In the scuffle, his finger caught my necklace. Suddenly my pearls were scattering across the floor. The creamy beads I loved so much were rolling away from me into shadowed corners. My deepest fear became my present reality. My life was the broken necklace, with pieces of my soul bouncing uncontrollably to destinations unknown. I could no longer suppress the emotions I'd kept inside for so long. I burst into tears and dove to the floor in an attempt to recover what I could save, none of which was my dignity. I was naked from the waist up, sprawled out on the floor picking up pearls, picking up pieces of my mother, pieces of Joanie and pieces of me. I was sobbing uncontrollably, and felt the mascara streaming down my cheeks. What was I going to tell our son? I was a complete failure.

I could sense Ron's scorn as he watched me down on all fours, begging and pleading to be loved. He turned and left the dining room. I heard the front door close. I felt as if someone else I loved had died. I knew my marriage was fatally damaged and beyond repair.

The four letters A-T-C-G came to my mind again.

Annie Too Can Grovel.

Annie Too Could Grasp.

I stopped. "Annie, get a hold of yourself," I said aloud. I then sat in silence for the longest time. I wiped away my tears and ruined makeup. I took a deep breath and exhaled. I pushed negative thoughts out of my mind. I vowed I would make an effort to remain positive. I said a prayer and asked for guidance — I asked for peace. Strangely enough, I felt a presence of strength. I smiled. I looked around the room, thinking, at least I am still alive.

Almost with hope, I crawled across the floor, searching for each missing pearl. To some, my necklace was only little round beads on a string. To me, my necklace was the symbol of my family tree. The pearls could be restrung; I would wear the necklace again. But can a flaw in genetic code be repaired? Probably not. I believed that if I could somehow prove that a genetic mutation existed, it might save other women from enduring the torture that accompanied hereditary breast cancer. It might even save their lives. I had to find evidence that it was real. I had to put together the pieces of an impossible puzzle. I had to find a way to decode a mutation in the double helix. I had to decode myself.

A-T-C-G.

Analyze The Catastrophic Gene.

Extract from *Ann Parker Decoded*, Brampton, ON: Annie Parker Books, 2014

When Annie Parker was fourteen years old, she lost her mother to cancer. Twelve years later, her beloved sister, Joan, also died from the same disease. Annie's doctors told her it was "just bad luck." She didn't believe them. Annie became convinced that there had to be a genetic link and that she, too, would get cancer.

She did. When she was twenty-nine, Annie developed breast cancer. She survived; her marriage didn't. Then, nine years later, Annie was diagnosed with Stage 3 ovarian cancer; once again she survived.

Meanwhile, Dr. Mary-Claire King, a geneticist at the University of California, Berkeley, discovered the BRCA1 gene mutation responsible for 5 to 10 percent of all breast cancers. Annie became one of the first women in Canada to be tested for the mutation and her results were positive for the deadly gene.

In 2006, Annie had cancer for the third time. She survived and has become an advocate for cancer awareness and genetic testing.

Annie's life story was the inspiration for the award-winning film *Decoding Annie Parker* (2014) starring Samantha Morton, Helen Hunt and Aaron Paul.

Radiant

Miranda Pearson

In his white coat the radiologist jokes:
we're in the bat cave up here.

The dark room, its thick metal door. And when inside,
a sense of backstage, of secrecy — the table in the centre

a slab where you might expect Frankenstein, hair on end,
pink and green smoke spiralling from his test tubes.

You climb on, compliant, and they begin their measuring, their
math-chat, red lights tack your torso as if for a plane's landing.

You are a runway. Bisected and branded
you keep still. Stretch your arms behind to hold the pole,

brace like a stripper — your exposed breasts
scarred like hers, too. The machine's swivelling eye

directs itself and when it's turned on
the red buzzer blares its loud applause —

how well you receive this toxic cure,
how well you hold the pose.

LEARNING TO NOT LAUGH IT AWAY

Francine Cunningham

My relationship with my breasts is almost as varied as the names that can be attached to them: boobs, jugs, sweater stretchers, my shelf, ode to joys, my girls, my fluffy pillows. Not too long ago, I remarked to a friend that I wished that I could take off my boobs whenever I choose, like parts from a machine, set them high on a shelf until I need them next. My breasts are large enough that I can only shop for bras in select stores and they cost upwards of seventy dollars — it seems reasonable to wish I could just have a break from them now and then.

Growing up, my mom and aunties would pull me aside, whisper in low voices, "Are you sure you shouldn't look at getting them reduced? They really are too big for a girl of your age. You don't need that type of attention from boys, you know." I can tell you that as a teenager this doesn't give you the sort of confidence you hope for.

But now I'm an adult and when they ask, they frame the question around thoughts of my health instead. "Your back will feel so much better. You know when you have babies they'll just get bigger. Why are you still looking for that kind of attention from men?" Well — almost always around my health.

I don't see how my boobs, and the size of them, should be anyone else's problem. Why should I have to be defined by them? But from the moment that I realized I had breasts, they have played a big role in my identity as a woman.

❧

The first realization that my breasts were going to be things to which I gave more than a cursory amount of attention came to me in junior high gym class. Don't all the best school war stories come from gym class? It was trampoline day. I bet you can guess how this is going to go. Up until that afternoon I thought I was just like every other girl in my class. I had never really thought about my body as anything other than like everyone else's. I knew that most of the girls in my class were still in training bras and that I was wearing a double-D bra, the kind I had to buy from Sears with my mom. But it had not occurred to me to mind the difference. It didn't trouble me, and it wasn't important.

So there I was, in the middle of the black mesh, straining to go higher and higher. The gym was old, with beams that stretched across the ceiling. Dangling in the corners were ropes that almost touched the floor, against the walls leaned folded-up bleachers made of wood, painted on the wall behind the basketball hoop was our school mascot in blue and gold. But none of that mattered to me. That day all I wanted was to jump so high that I brushed my fingers across the dusty steel beams. I could feel them, my classmates' eyes, as they marvelled at how high I was jumping, their hands clutched around the metal, feeling each of my bounces running through their bodies. I thought I heard a gasp and smiled wider, I was almost there, but then I heard it again and as the sound became louder I realized it wasn't gasps of shock and awe, but laughter. I glanced down, a ring of red-faced kids with grinning mouths and wide eyes were pointing at me. Their laughter echoed around the mostly empty gymnasium. I slowed down, unsure of what was happening. I looked for my best friend, Danni, but the boy she had a crush on had his arm around her shoulders and was laughing into her ear. She gave me a wavering smile before joining in, stretching out her arm and giggling. I didn't know why. That was until three boys to my left started miming my bouncing boobs. I stopped jumping. I stood in the centre of that mesh and stared into Danni's eyes. I could feel my T-shirt clinging to my body and red heat flooding my face. The sound of all that laughter pushed me off the trampoline. Once I hit the floor I ran to the change room. Pulled on a sweater and sat on the bench in the corner, mopping up my tears with the grey corner of my sleeve and hating with every fibre of my being the body I had no control over.

After that I started to wear baggy T-shirts. Started to shop from the men's department. Oversized hoodies. Anything to hide. And then suddenly there were even more differences between me and the other girls. I started to notice them all over. The other girls shaved past their knees. The other girls wore eyeliner and mascara. The other girls were proud of the tiny breasts that filled out their spaghetti-strapped tank tops. But they were allowed to be proud. Mine were too big, too different.

In high school I was still self-conscious. But I also wanted to be sexy. Kind of. And I knew that boobs meant sexy. So I started to wear tank tops, V-neck white T-shirts that showed off my bra, and I was happy for the attention. But I still always had a hoodie on hand. I was ready to hide at any moment.

And there were growth spurts in high school. From double-D to G. With the growth spurts came stretch marks. Just another thing to make me different. I was the only girl in high school who had them, or at least it felt that way. So now I had big boobs, the wavering confidence that showed itself in flaunting them/hiding them, and stretch marks. Let's just say it was a weird time when it came to boys.

But also girls. Sleepovers. Those magical weekend nights that taught you what it meant to be a woman, sort of. Starting off the night were movies and pizza, laughter and impromptu makeup lessons, and then everyone madly changing into PJs for the serious business of talking about boys. The feeling of undressing in front of them. Knowing that their eyes would be on my body, telling myself it didn't matter, who cared anyways because we were all just girls, but knowing that things were always just a little bit different. My shirt slipped over my head and in that brief darkness I heard a tinkle of laughter. My face burned red but I had no choice now. I pulled it off the rest of the way and stuck my chest out in mock courage. But they weren't laughing at me, they were giggling because they were nervous, at least I think that's why. And then one asked, in a wavering voice, if I loved how big my boobs were. And another chimed in with how she wished hers were bigger and she could never wear bras like me. The girl closest to me asked if she could feel them, just for a second, because she would never have ones like mine. And then they were all around me, comparing mine to theirs. But how could I tell them that I wished I didn't have them and that all I wanted to do was put my shirt on and go back to gossiping and that no, I didn't let boys touch them and that they actually hurt sometimes and could we please stop. Instead I nodded and pretended that everything was okay and slept with my bra on even though it hurt.

❧

And then I was old enough to drink. To do drugs and go dancing. To let boys I didn't know put their arms around me. Whisper into my ear. Try to sleep with me. Push-up bras had entered the picture. I was eighteen and couldn't wait to go to clubs. I was living away from home and I was independent. I was ready to do whatever I wanted and I was ready to be sexy, to leave my hoodie at home.

Roving hands in the strobe lights. Hands I didn't know. Rough, older. They filled themselves with my boobs. They squeezed while a man leaned in and marvelled into my ear, slurred words that made me feel embarrassed. I pulled away but he held on. Invited his friends over to have a try. I pushed against their shoulders but they laughed and held my arms behind my back. Each took a handful. Took the size of my boobs as an unspoken invitation.

Twisting, I tried to hide. Wished for the hoodie I left at home. The grabbing. The squeezing. The laughing. The assault. It only stopped when someone pulled them away and grabbed my hand, pulled me through the mess of sweaty people. To the dark corner where you had to scream to be heard. It was a man who I had never seen before. He asked if I was okay. I nodded. I liked the way his grin made the skin around his eyes crinkle. The way the scruff on his chin felt as he leaned in to tell me I was beautiful.

I crossed my arms over my chest. He winked and leaned in again, pushed his mouth against mine. I didn't owe him anything but he thought I did. He put a hand up my shirt, tried to shove it under my bra. I slapped his face. Surprised, he yanked my hand away and held it behind my back. I slapped him with my other hand. He grinned and shoved his mouth against mine again. A friend finally found me. Tears were running black down my face. She took me away from the loud music. The breath laced with beer.

My friends and I laughed it away later the next day. After mascara had been washed off cheeks and war stories told and retold. But then it happened again. Not the man in the club with the scruff on his chin and sweet words, I never saw him again, but with different men, different laughs, different roving hands not waiting for an invitation.

Eventually I stopped drinking. Stopped going to clubs. Slowly, I learned not to laugh it away.

In my twenties I was tired of the attention. I learned how to ignore the way some people didn't look at my face. The way their eyes roved over my chest instead. In the office I dressed like all the other office ladies. At least that's what it felt like to me. Pencil skirts and blouses, blazers and sweaters. In my mind I was in the generic office uniform and for a while felt safe in it. Until one day my boss pulled me aside, early into my job, and told me to think about wearing tops that were less revealing. I wanted to say, I'm sorry that the fact I have boobs is distracting for you but maybe you should look to yourself first and not me. But I was shy so I said, "Okay," before pulling on my jacket over my blouse. I started to dress in cable knit cardigans, wrapped billowing multicoloured scarves around my neck and shoulders, just as long as it was something to pull over my boobs.

From my desk I could overhear the guys in the office where they gathered outside the conference room to talk. If I swivelled my head I could see them, like a pack, vibrating with young energy.

They were each always so eager to up the others, become the alpha. I heard my name one day. "How could you not like her, I mean…" and then they all started laughing. I peeked over at them. The speaker was a tall guy near my age, his hands made motions like mountains over his chest. My face turned red as they all started to laugh. I pulled my cardigan tighter, wished for a hoodie from my younger days.

＊＊

But then something happened, as I got older, as the women in my life matured around me. As we began to stop comparing our bodies to each other's and started to relish what made us unique. I began to realize that my boobs were so much more than pieces of a puzzle I wished I could take a break from.

It's not that I stopped having interactions around my boobs, that the occasional comment about their size or laughter meant to hurt me didn't happen, because they did and do, but it's just now, I don't hate my body that I can't control because of them.

On the day I went to see my sister after she had gotten back from the hospital after giving birth to her first child I remember how tired she was. She was propped up in bed with this goofy smile on her face. Her hair was flung around in a jumbled mess around her head and there was residue from tears around the edges of her eyes. I crept into her room and sat perched on the bed beside her. The room was warm with the strength of summer's sun and I wanted to go open a window, to let out the stuffiness, but she wouldn't let me. The baby sleeping in the tiny bed beside her snored into the musty heat. As long as he was content she was content. We chatted in that afternoon heat in slow sentences, turning our gaze from each other to his little face. Until he woke up, his little lips puckering and his fists grasping at air. My sister pulled down her tank top until her boob poked out. She gave me an "oops, shit, you're here" smile and chuckle before shrugging her shoulders and picking up her new baby. Her breasts were large, swollen with milk. She positioned his head against her left breast and sighed when he finally latched on. She leaned back and cradled his head, her eyes telling the story about how much in love she was. And I realized something, that my breasts were more than all the experiences I'd had. They were me.

I thought about how mine warn me of my approaching period. Getting tender on the sides. How throwing off my bra at the end of the day is a ritual that feels so good. I thought about how they felt under the fingertips of someone caressing them in love and how they filled out that perfect black dress. I also thought about that tendril of fear as I saw women with scars where theirs used to be or when I heard of women being put into the ground because of the lumps that grew undetected for too long.

❦

I am no longer self-conscious about the silver stripes that crisscross along my skin from those early growth spurts. I am confident enough in myself to know that sometimes boobs are just annoying. Sometimes they make you feel sexy. Sometimes people will be jealous. One day they'll be used to feed my children. Sometimes people will take the size of them as an invitation. But mostly, I've come to know that these flying saucers, holy grails, jogging partners — are mine. And that's okay.

THE EXHIBITIONIST

Emily Davidson

Natalie's breasts are the stuff of legends. They are the kind of breasts that make an entrance, descend the curved staircase, one gloved hand on the railing. Natalie's breasts are Christina Hendricks breasts, Kat Dennings breasts, Kate Winslet breasts. They are divas. Natalie's breasts are power and responsibility. Natalie's breasts are E-cup miracles. They are the python in *The Jungle Book* whispering *trust in me*.

⇥⇤

The first time I meet her, Natalie scares the living daylights out of me. It is 2009; we've both just moved into graduate student housing at the University of British Columbia. I'd arrived, alone, several days before, and our introduction is a rushed greeting with her parents in tow. My roommate, it turns out, is a beautiful redhead with a face like a Botticelli painting and the figure to match. She drops her possessions in her room and walks into mine.

"Your room is much bigger," she says.

I don't know what to say to this. I am a tall mouse.

"I don't mind switching," I manage. "We could talk to the office in the morning."

"Oh, I'm not staying here tonight," she says. "We're staying in a *hotel*." The word hotel sounding like *country club* or *first class* or *obviously*.

After she leaves, I call my mother and confess that I'm going to have to move out. I can't live with this astonishing Elizabethan monarch with her vastly perfect breasts.

I was raised by a modest mother. Spaghetti straps were not allowed; bared midriffs and clingy garments were discouraged. If she had ever purchased me a two-piece swimsuit, it was before I hit puberty, and probably at a second-hand store. Either by nature or as a result of my environment, I too was a modest dresser: the one time I flouted the rules — by wearing a spaghetti-strap top under a sweater to a grade-seven dance, and then tucking my sweater into a friend's locker — I felt so naked and ashamed I spent the entire dance with my arms wrapped around my torso.

I appreciated my breasts mostly because not having them was worse. Having breasts meant the boys had bra bands to snap while they waited behind you in line. Having breasts meant your girlfriends didn't grill you in gym class for having nothing worth strapping down. Breasts meant you were keeping up, not exactly a late bloomer, not exactly the success of those girls who grew first and biggest. Breasts at the right rate meant invisibility. I kept up, but not too much.

At our first class, Natalie introduces me to everyone as her wife. It turns out we're in the same department — Creative Writing — and so besides living with her, we also have several classes together. I laugh to show she is kidding.

I quickly learn that attending campus events with Natalie is like going to a moth festival next to an open flame. She turns heads. It's not just the breasts — it's the cheekbones and the plush mouth and the hair the colour of burnished copper. One of our earliest outings is a poetry reading at the graduate student union building, in a humid room on the second floor that smells of baked linoleum. After the reading, when it becomes acceptable to mingle and drink, I see one of the handsome men in our department angle toward us. He dips his head to Natalie, careful to catch the low tones of her voice. They go to a corner of the room, Natalie and the handsome man, and have a conversation that lasts the entire evening. When I glance over from time to time, she is laughing or leaning very close or nursing her glass. At the end of the night they part with promises to get coffee, and I make a checkmark next to his name on my mental list of people who noticed Natalie and not me.

I go home wishing I were different. Wishing, for perhaps the first time consciously, to be seen.

❦

Natalie develops the habit of bursting into my room at the end of her day to tell me every thought she's had since we last saw each other. I am usually mid-project when this happens, and rising to meet her is like trying to have a conversation while surfacing from a deep-sea dive. I am still wearing the wetsuit and her words are all rubbery.

It is determined that we should go swimming while the weather holds. The air is warm with the turn in it that signals autumn, and I wear a tankini that hides only some of what I want to hide, but is daring for the simple fact that the top and bottom don't meet. There is so much skin — upper legs, gasp! Shoulders and sternum, gasp! — and I have to repress the urge to swim in my sundress. The beach is deserted, but still, someone might *see*.

It is built in, this instinct for self-protection. This shielding.

Natalie wears a blue polka-dot bikini that holds up her breasts like an offering. It's not the fault of the breasts, they're just made that way.

❦

The first thing people notice about my mother is a softness. A warmth, her tendency to bring baked goods or remember special events. She is truly kind, in a way that is probably old-fashioned. She is a safe person in a world full of shifters.

I do not think my mother likes her body, which, like her, is

106

soft. I have a suspicion that she hides it. I find this strange, as the person I like so much lives there.

><

The first term wraps with a residence gala. A number of the college women gather in our apartment to primp, my room turning into a swath of skirts and curling irons. I am already dressed in a purple print dress with detachable straps very much attached. Natalie is missing, so I drift to her room to look for her.

She stands near the doorway, checking herself in the mirror. She has wiggled into a black sheath with a smooth line of cleavage at the neck. She is more *Mad Men* than *Mad Men*.

She turns to me and strikes a pose.

"Too much boob?" she says.

I look her over. Her breasts are resplendent.

"No," I say. "Although I kind of want to motorboat you right now."

She laughs. She leans over to put on a pair of black heels, and I realize it's been a long time since she scared me.

"I wish I had your boobs," I say.

She stands straight and shrugs. "Yeah, but I've been sexualized by people since I was like, nine. So there's that."

I look at her face. It is closed.

"There's that," I agree.

She grabs a clutch from the pile on her floor.

"What is even happening with those straps?" she says, pointing to my dress.

"They're keeping up my dress?" I say.

"No straps," she says.

I sneak back to my room and, behind the noise of misting hairspray, remove the straps and stuff them in a drawer.

We go to dinner. We whisper through the speeches. Natalie determines which college men she is going to set me up with. Natalie includes me in all of her jokes. I bask in her glow. It's the kind of glow that grows outwards, curved and welcoming. Afterwards, there is dancing, and we bounce around like teenagers, our shoes tossed in some lost elbow of the room.

I feel the presence of my bare shoulders all evening, but by halfway through the night, it isn't unpleasant anymore.

❦

As soon as she has children or ages past forty, Natalie's breasts are going to drop like stones, she tells me. Right to there, she says, pointing at a spot on her stomach. So she's going to have them reduced. She's already got it all planned. They're nice and all, but they're heavy. They're a weight.

❦

I take an undergraduate acting class as an elective. We spend a lot of the class lying on the floor making vowel sounds. We practise bits of Shakespeare, usually with something thrown in — *Hamlet* while gyrating, *Romeo and Juliet* with our heads on a partner's thigh. We walk around the room in different attitudes, practising awareness and copying our neighbours' gaits.

We are in the middle of an exercise, and I am working myself up to go next. I speak a line of dialogue, feel I could have done better, and say as much. My instructor gives me the eye.

"Stop apologizing," she says. "Do it again."

I speak the line of dialogue, followed by an instinctual "sorry."

"Again," she says.

It takes me four tries to get through without excusing myself.

❦

I call Natalie after class. She is on a bus. We chitchat for a while before she notices that I am crying. She asks me what's wrong, and I tell her about the acting session, about how everyone else in the class is so free. They don't care that they look like idiots reciting *Hamlet* with pelvis thrusts. They don't mind making mistakes or being exposed. Natalie commiserates while I have a slow and dawning epiphany. There is a pause in the conversation while I gather my courage and Natalie pulls the bell for her stop.

"I don't like myself," I realize.

"I know, sweet pea," she says.

"You like yourself."

"I do. And I think you are magnificent."

"I don't feel magnificent."

"I know."

We end the call, and I email a friend for a therapist recommendation.

My breasts are likely to deflate with age. Like melting Hershey's Kisses. Or meringues. But before then, I want to come to terms with their polite existence. The ways in which they haven't yet let me down. I want to live all the way through this body, as an extension and a pleasure. I want to be okay with my own glow, the softness of it, the way it is subtle and not insignificant.

Natalie drops into my room around dinnertime, where I am changing from one outfit to another. It has been a long day, and I am ready for comfort.

"Look away for a sec," I say, pulling my shirt over my head.

"I've seen your boobs already," she declares, picking over some articles of clothing I've tossed on the bed. "They're so sweet. Like two little apples."

I finish strapping myself in, realizing there is a note of envy in her voice. Not true jealousy — Natalie loves everyone and herself too much to wish anything different — but a wistfulness. Her breasts have determined so much about her life. Natalie, I realize, has never once been invisible. Never wielded obscurity like an inverse superpower.

I wonder if I can lend her some of what I am in the midst of shedding.

I buy a black strappy top with a low neck. It is silky, elegant. Cut for smallness. My breasts, too, are elegant. Audrey Hepburn breasts, Cate Blanchett breasts, Carey Mulligan breasts. My breasts are a sly wink, a promise. Smooth stretches of cresting skin. My breasts are B-cup miracles. A bashful forest creature you can call Flower, if you want to. I don't mind.

YOUR BODY IS GROWING

Laura Ritland

When we were ten years old, our bodies were taken
and framed in the faux wood of our classroom TV.
We sat before the film with the focused dread

of spring bulbs in the semi-dark while a voice like plastic wrap
described which parts of us would bleed or swell
and we crushed our knees more tightly into our chests:

in this fashion, we'd stop ourselves from learning the names
sliced over those pink diagrams. We'd silence
the static buzzing through our fronts at night,

uproot the buds growing through our flesh.
Pain was our allegiance. We each defined
how it felt. Yet when the film shrunk

to a seed and the lights turned on, we saw
each others' shared look of shame and rose as one
throbbing garden to our desks. We didn't know then

our bodies would become famous: bikini catalogues,
bathroom talk, mall windows and their women's breasts
propped like porcelain in glass cabinets.

LATE-BLOOMING BOOBIES

Valerie Hennell

The first thing I knew about breasts was that I didn't have any. What I had was an angry red gash between two tiny dots where nipples were supposed to be, covered by a huge itchy bandage.

It was 1960 and I was eleven years old, impatiently awaiting discharge from Vancouver General Hospital. Open heart surgery was new to Vancouver and my operation was a bit of an experiment: my surgeon perfected his technique on a poodle before fixing me.

Assisted by the new-fangled heart-lung machine, Dr. Robertson sawed through my sternum, opened my left ventricle, stapled my ribs back together and closed up my chest with eighteen black spidery stitches. Twenty-six days later, bedsore and restless, I just wanted out from under this huge stinky plaster so I could go home and learn to ride a bicycle.

Because now I was going to be normal. Now I could stop being the girl with the bad heart, watched over by nuns and forbidden all strenuous activity. Now I would grow and develop and maybe even have breasts like my big sister.

My parents were sailors so they sent me to the yacht club to recuperate. After seven years as a hot-house plant, I had no muscle tone and little coordination. With coke-bottle glasses and gangly everything, I was terrified of the wind, the sea, the boats and, most of all, the other kids.

After private school, boys were a heart-crushing novelty, and the girls — the girls all wore bras. Wouldn't they notice I didn't need one?

Apparently not. They were mesmerized by my scarlet zipper. They teased me incessantly and begged me to dive off the high dock to see if I would split open. Some of the boys threatened to push me. I felt like an alien and was treated like a mascot.

What was a tampon, anyway?

The other kids spoke in a laughing, jostling vernacular I didn't always understand. But one thing was certain: breasts were often mentioned and had a lot of different names.

Jugs, cans, boobs, titties… would I ever have some?

That summer "Itsy Bitsy Teenie Weenie Yellow Polka Dot Bikini" was the big hit on transistor radio. We knew all the words and sang it like an anthem. Bikinis were in! While other girls pranced around in hankies, I wore a one-piece tank suit and tried to always keep my shirt on.

As the weeks passed, sun and sea browned my skin and strengthened my muscles. When my first solo landing smashed into the dock (who knew you stop a sailboat by turning head to wind?) my nickname became Crash Hennell. It seemed like a badge of honour.

At least now my ugly flat chest was not the only focus of attention. As my confidence grew, I was increasingly determined to master this one-and-maybe-only-ever sport. Crash would show them! As my sailing skills increased, my fear began to evaporate.

And so it came to pass that one day as I pulled in the sheets and turned my ragged breast to the breeze, I realized I knew what I was doing. Somehow despite myself I had befriended the wind. I was in cahoots with an invisible force. I tightened the sails and headed for the horizon.

That year I grew through two sizes of swimsuits. Newly oxygenated blood swirled through my veins and swelled my flesh, but alas, not my mammaries.

In the privacy of our backyard I opened my shirt and turned my chest to the sun. The warmth felt miraculous as it licked at my shame and launched a lifelong propensity for tanning buck naked. I dreamed of the boys at the yacht club dreaming girl-dreams about me.

But who would ever love a scar-chest, tit-less, boob-less, flat-as-a-pancake?

By grade nine the popular girls wore smoothly bulging mohair sweaters! I had tiny breast-buds and extruding nipples that showed through my clothes. My mom took me to The Bay to buy a softly padded bra, and a boy I'd kissed at a party told the whole school that I wore falsies. Nothing crueller than puberty until old age!

I'm a grandmother now and this tale is being remembered over more than fifty years.

From the long view of elderhood it seems that after that summer Crash Hennell never looked back. A swimmer, a sailor, a sailing instructor, she won many regattas, outsmarting those boys on the downwind leg. She became editor of the paper, arts correspondent for the *Ubyssey*, broadcaster for CBC, record producer, writer and poet. She began writing her own novelty tunes.

What I lacked in muscle I made up for in wiles. What I'd lacked in cleavage, I was about to redeem. When I arrived at university, so did my boobies.

When my hormones caught up to me, I was suddenly voluptuous. Overnight my breasts became objects of admiration and attraction. Over several sun-kissed summers, my scar receded between two bulbous mounds of brown. Hardly anyone mentioned it anymore.

Before the ozone dissolved in a hole, I put myself through university teaching sailing on English Bay, wearing nothing but a bikini, a sun hat and a mahogany tan.

I turned down a job as a bra model and wore a bloody fish-skin corset cut for me by a Mexican fisherman. A friend built me a private patio at her house in the jungle so I could sun myself naked without making ado. Me gusta mi pubico!

Oddly, after all those years of not having any, breasts mattered very little to me. They were inconvenient. They caused a kerfuffle with menfolk. They made it uncomfortable to run and to lie on my stomach. They were heavy when unfettered and bras were such a pain.

I sometimes wondered why I was lugging these puppies around.

I found out when my son was born. Post-partum, my breasts were bigger than his head. I had so much milk that during three years nursing, I served as a wet nurse and suckled someone else's babe who was adopted at birth.

A couple of years later, a child I didn't know walked into the room and the milk in my breasts let down and spurted. It was the baby I'd nursed and hadn't seen since infancy. My breasts have their own secret wisdom.

After childbirth, my scar was all but forgotten. After a half century of near perfect health, it's a faded old friend that keeps me mindful of gratitude.

As my children succumb to the lure of tattoos, I rest in the knowledge that I have the ultimate tat between my tits.

I'm sixty-six now with many grandchildren. My late-blooming breasts have retired to more relaxed pastures.

Last summer my youngest granddaughter was perched on my tummy in the bathtub when I noticed her staring at my chest. I thought she was going to ask me about my scar, but she was lost in her own giggling wonder.

"Gra'ma Valley has big boobies!" she gurgled, patting them lovingly. "Will I have big boobies one day?"

BERRIES

Moni Brar

The story begins with a girl. She is ten years old, tilting her head and gently leaning into a half-broken barbed-wire fence. She doesn't mind how the barbs poke into her chest; her dirty T-shirt provides a thin barrier that's just enough to keep them from breaking open her skin. For some reason, the sharp stabs of pain make her feel better. They're like little pinpoints she can focus on. The sun beats down on her head and her face feels sticky. A fly buzzes near her ear but it feels like it's inside her head. Her thoughts compete with the incessant buzz. She contemplates whether to squeeze through the barbed wire to take the shortcut through the neighbour's strawberry field or to go to the road and take the long way around. She loves cutting through the strawberry field and hopping over the narrow rows of plants that are so shiny and full they almost look fake. If she is quick and no one is around, she can usually sneak in a few strawberries. Looking down at the glass bowl she's holding, she decides it's safer to take the long route. That way, none of the steaming dahl will spill and she won't get in trouble from her mother.

As she walks toward the neighbour's house, her pace slows and each step feels heavier, as though she's trudging through the dahl itself. She keeps her eyes downcast and wills each foot to move forward. She wishes her mother would stop sending her on these trips, shoving her out the door to deliver a portion of food carved out of whatever she's cooked that day. She has become the reluctant delivery girl for a stream of samosas, pakoras, dahls and subjis. It's bad enough that every now and then, she has to deliver it to the German family at the end of street, where it's both offered and accepted with an equal amount of awkwardness and embarrassment. But this delivery is much worse.

116

I realize I'm standing at the door of the neighbour's house, but I don't remember the actual walk there. I hesitate before knocking on the door and pray that no one will be home. Please god, please god, please god. I chew on my lower lip. I taste blood. I knock and all too quickly, the wooden door swings back and there's Auntie smiling at me from behind the screen door. My heart sinks.

"*Behta*!" Auntie exclaims. She always uses this term of endearment. Everything about Auntie is round — her body is round, her glasses are round, and behind them, her eyes are getting rounder and rounder as she stares at the bowl. She smooths down her shirt over her fat belly and anxiously leans forward to peer into the bowl. She hurriedly opens the screen door and says, "*Aja, aja!*" Come in, come in! A flurry of words washes over me. Auntie wags her finger at me, admonishing me for my unruly dog. He came over again last night and stole her shoes from outside their door. She says she came by in the morning and retrieved two pairs of slippers and a running shoe, all of which the dog had safely stored in his house. I can see a pair of pink plastic slippers by the door, covered in a film of dried dog saliva. I secretly feel proud.

I stand very still on the steps and let the reprimands for my wayward dog wash over me. I intently look forward, past Auntie, into the dark house. Her voice sounds like a distant echo that's replaced the buzz in my head. I'm unable to speak, to move, to think. Auntie grabs hold of my arms, careful not to upset the big bowl of soupy lentils, and pulls me into the house. In one deft move, she snatches the bowl out of my hands and shoves me into the living room, promising to be back with some biscuits.

And there he is. He looks at me slyly, as though he's been expecting me. I consider bolting for the door, but as I turn, Auntie bustles back into the living room, biscuit-laden plate in hand, and continues to natter on about the damn dog.

"Go. Sit with your big brother. He wants to play with you." She nudges me forward, walks past and places the biscuits on the plastic-covered coffee table.

The fear bubbles up in my throat. Words can't be formed. This man frightens me. I want to scream, "He's NOT my brother!" but I'm completely incapacitated. I know what's going to happen next. It's the same every time.

"Ma, can you make me some chai? Brew it extra long, though. I like it strong," he says with a smirk, staring at me. His eyes rake up and down my body, resting on my breasts. His eyes bore into my breasts and his smile turns into a lip-smacking sneer. Even though I'm fully dressed, I feel as if he can see through my clothes. I cross my arms across my chest, trying to hide my breasts. I hate them. I think to myself that if I didn't have breasts, none of this would be happening.

"Go on. Don't be so shy. You play while I go and make the chai," Auntie says obliviously as she leaves the room.

As soon as his mother has left, he comes at me. He grabs my thin wrists and drags me back to the big recliner he was sitting in. He props me up on his knee. I know not to squirm. It only makes things worse. His big hands are all over me. I can feel his prickly face against my neck as he fondles me, rubbing me into his lap. His hands are on my breasts, massaging them, tweaking my nipples. His breath is sour and hot as he rubs my breasts, and he whispers hoarsely, "lily-white, lily-white," in his meager English with a thick Indian accent. I don't know why he says this or what it means. I stare at the Bollywood movie playing on the old TV in front of me. A big-bosomed actress is lip-syncing a Hindi song as she runs through a field of saffron, looking coyly at the camera, breasts heaving. I feel his hands twisting my own breasts. His hands feel big and rough, and my breasts feel smaller and smaller, and more and more raw. I feel dirty. Ugly. I wish I didn't have breasts. I feel ashamed of them. My body goes limp, my mouth slackens, my eyes unfocus. I give up. Everything vanishes into a pinpoint.

⋘⋙

She is at home, standing in the bathroom. She lifts her T-shirt over her head and looks at herself in the mirror. She hates the white undershirt she's wearing. It looks like a boy's. She watches her chest heaving in the mirror. She thinks of the Bollywood actress's heaving chest, but her own doesn't look anything like that. Hers is heaving because she's crying and trying not to make a sound. She knows that if anyone finds out what's happening, it will be her fault. She will get in trouble. She will get slapped and yelled at by her mother. She is only ten but she knows this as a fact.

She lifts her undershirt over her head. She sees the bruises starting to form, the size of a man's fingerprints. But she chooses not to look at these and focuses on her breasts instead. They look so small and ugly. They are brown — though not as brown as her hands and arms that have become darker and darker this summer. She turns and looks at her profile in the mirror. Her breasts are barely a bump on her chest. She turns again and looks straight on. She wipes her arm across her face, smearing the tears. She focuses on the marks the barbed wire has left. A scratch here, a cut there, across her chest. She thinks her breasts deserve this punishment. Even though they're small, she wishes they didn't exist. Maybe then, he wouldn't do the things he does to her.

At school, someone in her grade five class recently said it looked like she had two peas on a board. A few of the other kids laughed. Her best friend, Sandra, quickly came to her defence and said something smart and funny and that shut everyone up. She wishes she could remember what Sandra said so she could say it herself, but she can't remember because the buzzing in her head was too loud. She thinks about the decaying magazines she found with Sandra recently on one of their bike adventures to an old abandoned barn in someone's pasture. Flipping through the half-rotten pages, they could make out pictures of naked women. They had big, round breasts, like perfect milky-white globes. Sandra seemed unfazed by the pictures, but she was mesmerized. Is this what her breasts were supposed to look like? If she had breasts like these, would she be beautiful? Would bad things stop happening to her? Or would more bad things happen to her? It's hard to tell.

—◆—

I wait for the click before I let out my breath.

I hear it now, the sharp metallic signal telling me that he has left the apartment. I walk from the kitchen to the living room and down the hall, my fingers lightly trailing along both walls, my eyes focused forward and refusing to take in the framed portraits lining the way, until I reach the front entrance.

Here the soft carpet gives way to ceramic tiles that are cold on my bare feet and make me even more aware of the goose-bumps tracking down my arms. I feel cold. Slowly pressing my eye to the keyhole, I make sure the hall outside is vacant. And then I do what has now become mindless habit, reaching down, one hand on the door handle and the other on the heavy lock; I unlock and then lock it. Doing it once again to be sure it really is locked. *Click-click*. Not realizing that, again, I've been holding my breath, I let out a sound, half sigh and half choked breath.

I return to the kitchen, but now my steps are swift and sure. Passing through the hall, this time I look directly at the portraits and frown at them. I'm not entirely sure why I keep them hanging up. There I am, captured in full wedding portrait glory — but strangely, not draped in traditional crimson silks, no heavy gold bangles from wrist to elbow, no hennaed hands politely folded, and no hair parted with a line of vermilion, the mark of a married Indian woman.

The version of me in the photos looks back at me, in off-white cotton much to the dismay of my mother, face scrubbed clean, without adornment or refinement. I look at this image of my painfully thin, small-breasted self. What I hate most about these photos is my eyes — so demure, so hopeful. So trusting. I look with disdain at my old, naïve self. What a fool, I think. With a quick shake of my head, I return to the kitchen and yank open the fridge door. I survey the disorganized contents and spot what I'm looking for. I grab the container of blueberries and quickly head back down the hall to the bathroom.

In the bathroom, I set down the blueberry container on the cluttered countertop. The first few times I did this, I immediately felt guilty for bringing food into the bathroom and could imagine my mother's disapproving response. *"Arre! Eh kee?"* Yes, Mother. *"Oh! What's this?"* Food in the bathroom! Unthinkable! That initial guilt quickly turned into a feeling of satisfied rebellion. A small, secret and insignificant rebellion, but a rebellion all the same.

⚛

This has become ritual. Each time he comes unbidden and unannounced, uses her body and leaves her to piece herself together again. She tells herself that this is her punishment for leaving him. That she has broken the cardinal rule in an Indian marriage — a woman must stay with her husband no matter what. She has countless Indian friends who continue to uphold this rule. Despite abuse, indifference or incompatibility, they stay in their marriages, bowing to tremendous familial, cultural or community pressure. She frequently alternates between envying and resenting these friends. Are they stronger than her and able to persevere where she failed? Or are they just too weak and submissive to stand up for themselves? She imagines that the answer may lie between the two.

In any event, she herself feels like a contradiction of strength and weakness. He comes to punish her almost on a weekly basis, and she willingly accepts the punishment he doles out, which is usually a combination of a verbally abusive tirade and sexual assault — both of which leave her feeling empty, worthless and ashamed. While she had the strength to leave him over six months ago, the deeply ingrained guilt she feels for doing this now leaves her silently allowing him to abuse her. She's come to resign herself to this fate and views his abuse as some sort of penance. While intellectually she knows this is a distortion of the truth and that what's happening is unacceptable, emotionally she's ensnared in feeling that she has utterly failed as a wife.

⋙

I plug the bathtub, run the water and check the temperature. While the bathtub fills, I turn my back to the mirror and start to undress. I can't bear to face the mirror. I went to pray at the gurudwara this morning and am still wearing my traditional Indian clothes. First, I remove the chunni from my head. I'm surprised it's still there, given the violence of the sex I didn't really want to have with him. The long, translucent stretch of fabric slips from my fingers and falls to the floor. I then remove my kameez, gently lifting it overhead as I can feel the bruises starting to form on my breasts where he gripped me and held me down. I untie the string that gathers my salwar at my waist and release it. With a swoosh, the silky fabric pools at my feet. I look down at the colourful fabrics, admiring how festive and happy they look and what a stark contrast this is to how I feel in this moment. I step over the pile of clothes, slip off my underwear, and grab the blueberry container.

After gingerly testing the temperature with a toe, I lower my body into the warm water. Resting the blueberry container on the corner of the bathtub, I remove a single blueberry and pop it into my mouth. I revel in the perfect roundness of it. I close my eyes and slide my body underwater. Calmness envelops me. I feel aware of my entire body, feel in control of each and every single cell. The water pushes into my ears, heavy against my eyelids, moves between my toes. Each strand of my hair feels taut and separated. I gently move my arms in the water and feel the resulting swirls against my body. I rest my hands on my broken breasts and sink into their painful ache. I can feel the bruises he has left — thumb, finger, finger, finger, pinky. The deep purple imprints are the remnants of him tugging and twisting the soft tissue, as if he's trying to pry them completely off my chest. His anger seems to zero in on my breasts. I wonder if it has anything to do with the fact that these breasts are not the ones he has longed for all his life. These are not the ones in the magazines he carelessly stashes under his bed. These are not the milky-white, pink-topped breasts of his boyhood fantasies, like some tantalizingly lewd confection. Rather, these are too-small breasts, with dark, ugly brown nipples.

I push the cold blueberry against the roof of my mouth and feel it burst. It's like a little explosion in my head. The skin tastes slightly sour, and the sweetness of the flesh fills my mouth. This is my escape. For the few moments I'm underwater, I feel whole. I am untouchable. The bruises vanish, his scent gets washed away, the pain in my breasts is soothed, and my shame dissolves. I can imagine a different life. One where I am safe and free. One where I have more little liberties. Where I am able to dress the way I want, choose my own friends, go where I want, and be the person I want to be — confident, respected and cherished.

I come up every few moments to place a fresh blueberry in my mouth and then return underwater. I roll the blueberry around on my tongue, testing myself to see how long I can wait to give in to the temptation to press it against the roof of my mouth. Each little blueberry is a small miracle to me — so tiny, but so exquisitely powerful. The taste fills me with nostalgia for a simpler time and place. It reminds me of childhood summers where I, along with my siblings, would be filled with anticipation and, eventually, squeals of delight for the season's first blueberries, or my secret shortcuts through the strawberry fields. I marvel that things as simple as berries were able to bring me so much joy. I yearn for that simplicity, and more so, for that all-consuming joy.

I rest underwater a moment longer. My body is not limp, my mouth is not slack. My eyes are closed, but everything is in focus. I am submersed, cleansed and calm.

Underwater, I feel in control of my body and mind and with each blueberry popping in my mouth, I'm reminded of many long-forgotten joys. I cup my breasts, my broken breasts, caress them, and let the water soothe them. They may not be perfect, but they are mine.

BREASTS

Susan Glickman

I hated them from the start —
they burned, they poked,
two scoops of humiliation
disgracing my unused chest.

I used to lie on my stomach praying
"Please don't grow" but they did,
faster than anyone else's,
sending me back to school hunched,
clutching books between belly and chin.
Unbalanced in ballet, red-faced at gym, shy
in the showers —
shy everywhere, in fact, behind those twin announcements
that I was now a public target — fair game
to the rude boys smoking behind the school,
street-corner wankers,
someone's drunk uncle at a wedding,
someone's father.

They liked them, the men, and let me know it.
This did not help.
Most were rough, grabbing handfuls
as though breasts were just stuff, some stuff
they wanted, nothing to do with me.
Others were so serious, mammary scholars, all technique
and sincerity. Nipple-flickers. Lickers.
Ticklers.

So what.
The things just hung there, in my way,
flopping when I ran, aching every month,
useless. Until the babies came and then
such sweetness! I had never known such sweetness
as when my infants sucked and I could feel the milk
flowing down in little sparks as though it were pure
electricity, a current between us, and even my babies hummed
they were so happy and they stroked
my breasts.

And now I'm afraid
because they've outlasted their purpose,
and my friends are dying and it starts, here, in the breasts,
the milk curdled, sour, one spark
then a conflagration

and maybe they won't forgive me all those years
I hated them. Maybe they don't want to plough ahead
into years when no one leers or grabs;
years when everyone looks away.
Maybe they needed all that attention:
it kept them glossy and sleek, fat and purring
like ceremonial cats guarding the entrance
to an Egyptian tomb:

the right one named "Life,"
the left one "Death."

FEATHERS

Catherine Graham

She was a quiet woman, a keeper of secrets. Her hair, red all her life, even after it grew back in. They had to tell me before it happened. They couldn't keep her hair falling out a secret. I was eleven. We had recently moved to the quarry, the water-filled limestone pit that would forever haunt and comfort me.

"It's cancer, isn't it," I said, squeezing my schoolbooks tight to my new-budding chest. I'd just arrived home from school. They were sitting in the family room. Mom in her corner nook on the sectional chesterfield, her feet curled up, the black leather *Merck Manual* sitting open in the swan-neck curve of her athletic legs. Dad was sitting in the Windsor chair, recently refinished by Mom's determined and loving hands; the chestnut spindles caught the sudden cloud-breaking light as he leaned his tall body forward to rest his head on his hands. Like Mom he stared at the floor, the patterned carpet that held a collection of breadcrumbs from last night's dinner. They weren't surprised that I knew. None of us were. Even me, though the reality of my knowing became apparent only after I'd said those words.

Mom turned to me. "I'm sorry this had to happen to you."

But it didn't happen to me. It happened to you. My thoughts so loud I was sure she'd heard them.

＊＊

My mother's death at forty-eight put my then nineteen-year-old breasts on the radar. It began with self-checking. After lifting each arm, one at a time, I tamped each breast as my mother once tamped the dirt after planting pink petunias, tender and gentle around each freshly rooted stem. Tamp, tamp, tamp.

Then during my late twenties I had annual mammograms and ultrasounds. While sitting in the waiting room with the other women I was always the youngest.

With dense breasts I had my scares with lumps. I remember the panic and worry the first time I lay on my side in the half-lit ultrasound room, a pillow tucked behind me for support. When the technician pushed the cold hard device over the sensitive breast skin the insides of my jellied breast appeared on the black and white screen as a strange subterranean world. During this time I learned words like *fibroadenoma*. Friendly words. All encounters with lumps were benign.

After two decades of caution and negative results I got out of the habit of monthly examinations. It was summer 2012 and I was distracted by a writing project that wasn't going the way I'd hoped.

Then it was spring 2013 and news of Angelina Jolie's double mastectomy was everywhere including my morning paper — the news jolted me. How long had it been since I checked?

During my shower I restarted my routine. While moving the pads of my fingers over both breasts in a circular pattern I felt a pea-sized lump above the nipple of my left.

Fibroadenoma. Surely this was the answer.

The following week I lay on the hospital bed in my doctor's office, my left breast exposed to the bright cold air. I closed my eyes.

"Yes, it's probably nothing," she said, pressing her cool fingertips against the lump. "But you're due for a mammogram and ultrasound anyway."

I was ten in this memory. My mother was alive and well, standing by the kitchen sink, her hands immersed in the soapy dish water, scrubbing the bowl she'd used to make icing for cake, staring out the window at the ice-capped quarry. She'd given me the beaters to lick. I pushed my tongue between the metallic edges into the deeper places. I couldn't get enough of the sickly sweetness.

I followed her eyes to the flicker of movement in the bush. "What's that?" I asked. "A junco?"

"A chickadee."

I could never tell the little birds apart. The chickadees and juncos were both small and bouncy and mostly grey. Mom said I needed to pay closer attention, to spend more time seeing what was there, right in front of me.

Mom always noticed the small birds before I did. But with her as guide I learned to pay attention to details, however small, to help me tell the birds apart. I began to notice the markings of feathers, their colour and shape.

Her favourite was the cardinal. Not the male with his bright red showy feathers but the subdued female, her feathers a warm red-tinged brown.

Sometimes while playing outside I came across a feather lying on the ground. I picked it up and brought it back to Mom. She collected them in a vase by the windowsill. Blooms of feathery light.

I didn't worry while waiting for my family doctor's phone call with the mammogram and ultrasound results. I knew she'd say what she always did whenever she called. "Everything's fine."

But on this occasion she didn't say that. Instead she said, "We need to do a biopsy."

I wanted one done immediately but I was forced to wait. I was out of town for the week teaching a creative writing course.

I tried not to think about the ticking nipple time bomb lodged in my chest. I had a classroom full of students to teach for five full days. While driving down the tree-lined road to reach the Haliburton School of the Arts I heard my mother's voice. *I'm sorry this had to happen to you.*

❦

A week or so after the biopsy I was called back to the cancer hospital. Despite my polite insistence they wouldn't give me the results over the phone. I sat stiffly in the beige plastic chair waiting in the cold stark room. The painting of a pomegranate hung from the wall but it was an intrusion not a comfort. All those glossy red seeds — multiplying, dividing, spreading.

Finally the doctor came in the room. "The results show cancer," he said. He kept on talking after that but I did not hear a word.

Months later, I awoke in a stretcher in a post-op ward after someone shook my arm and said, "Catherine, wake up."

The voice was my mother's.

❦

Not long after that operation, I began noticing feathers during my walks around the city. I'd never noticed how abundant they were on sidewalks, streets and parking lots. Birds live all over the city of Toronto. Sparrows in cedars, seagulls circling over shops, pigeons in a flower-ring scrum pecking for bread, the machine-gun stutter of the cardinal. Feathers became my talismans during those long uncertain months.

One day while walking to Princess Margaret Hospital for my first radiation appointment I started counting the feathers. I saw so many along the way I lost count. It didn't matter. Each feather calmed me.

The radiation therapist made several marks on my skin. "These can be washed off," she said, "but the next ones will be permanent." She picked up a fine needle.

I thought of the neighbourhood I lived in. How it was filled with tattooed hipsters parading up and down the street, wearing ink proudly.

The procedure was quick as four pin pricks.

These dots will serve as compass points around my left breast, directional guides above my heart — north, south, east, west. They will map the next part of my cancer treatment — the radiation required to kill malignant cells and stop them from spreading.

"It's not so bad, right?" said the radiation therapist. She smiled and put down the needle. Without a mirror in the room I couldn't see the result. But out of the corner of my eye I spotted a dot the size of a freckle. I wondered if my mother had tattoos like these after her operation. Back in the '70s, did they mark the breast this way?

How strange to be diagnosed with the disease the exact age she died from it. Forty-eight. And yet despite the strangeness of the coincidence it was also a comfort. It seemed, to me, to bring us closer despite the fact she's been dead now for decades.

———

Finally the day arrived when my treatment came to an end. I sat in the same stark room where I'd received my breast cancer diagnosis. I angled my chair away from the painting of the pomegranate, those glossy seeds. To help ease the anxiety prickling through my body I thought of the feathers I'd encountered during my walks to and from Princess Margaret Hospital for treatment. I thought of my mother sitting in her corner nook on the chesterfield watching the birds gather at the feeder. Cardinals, chickadees, juncos.

Those previously unseen feathers I began noticing during that time had become comforting gifts, signs I was on the right path. Having spotted one I knew it was just a matter of time before I'd spot another. I was paying attention by seeing what was there, right in front of me. I was making my mind focus and gather to make sense of my life.

The door opened and the surgeon appeared. "Good news," he said. "The cancer is gone."

Months later towelling dry after a shower I caught my reflection in the mirror. A fleck of dirt would not come off. What the hell? I scrubbed hard with the edge of the terry towel and watched the pale skin beneath my clavicle rash red. The fleck remained. I checked my watch. I have no time for this. I have a class to teach. Leaving the dirt mark there — what else could I do? — I dressed for class.

I gathered handouts and lecture notes, locked the front door, and began my walk to U of T's St. George Campus. Rounding the first corner I saw a grey feather lodged in a sidewalk crack. The reality hit me: that fleck of dirt I'd seen earlier was ink. How could I forget?

I realized, then, the power of the mind to forget pain, to focus instead on the ordinary details of life. As if to drive the lesson home, a white feather drifted into my line of vision before floating to the ground.

So Big Men Can't Help Themselves

Sierra Skye Gemma

For the first eight years of my life, they call me Teeny because I am so small. No one knows that I don't get enough food. The only foods we ever seem to have around are noodles and pesto. And I hate pesto. If I complain, Mom says, "Again I tell you, it is easier for a camel to go through the eye of a needle than for a rich man to enter the kingdom of God," and I still believe her. I still believe everything the Jehovah's Witnesses tell me.

The kids at school call me Sierra Miller Mooser Pie, which doesn't even make sense. They call me Ski-Slope Nose and say I'm stuck up. They make up a song just for me. It goes, "Roses are red. Violets are black. Sierra's chest is as flat as her back." Then they laugh.

They invent that song because in fifth grade I am only fifty pounds and all legs and arms and a head too big for my body. In sixth grade, I am only sixty pounds and still no more than gangly limbs. When seventh grade comes, I have nothing but bloated nipples while my best friend, Cammie, is pushing into a B-cup. But during the summer before ninth grade, I go from almost nothin' to a C-cup. It happens so fast that I get stretch marks on the inner sides of my breasts.

No one can believe it. Other kids start a nasty rumour that I stuff my bra. Then one day, I go to the community pool. Some kids from elementary school are there and they can see me splashing in the water with my big, beautiful breasts. I think things will finally change, but the boys still see me as that weird, poor, Jehovah's Witness kid and nothing changes. Except for the name. They call me Sierra Mountains now and I think it's better than the other names, but I'm not sure.

When I am only twelve years old, and just out of seventh grade, my father stops sending me to school because he doesn't want the "bad boys" to know me. He thinks he should be the only man in my life. I start cleaning houses with my mom every Friday and she tries to pay me a little bit of her wages when she can. After my parents realize that they could get in big trouble for keeping me out of school, they don't send me back to public school. Too many boys there.

Instead, they find a free independent study program run by the school district. It's supposed to be for wayward teens, but I'm just a poor Jehovah's Witness kid. When we sign up for the program, my parents lie to the administrator, saying I was homeschooled during eighth grade and that they want to try something different for ninth grade. I work very hard to get good grades during that first year, and when I enter tenth grade at the age of fourteen, I finally feel like I've caught up after missing a whole year of school. I still work with my mom every Friday, but I find that most of my schoolwork is easy and I have plenty of time to do whatever I want. I know I can't ask my parents to do fun things, so I ask if I can get another job and they allow it.

I get my first real job at Hometown Deli and everything changes.

My boss, Ralph, has a wife and two kids. Ralph is thirty-six years old when he hires me just after my fifteenth birthday. People say Ralph used to be an actor on a soap opera, but my mom doesn't let me watch soaps so I don't know if that's true. In any case, I have a huge crush on him.

I love working at Hometown Deli for so many reasons: I make more money than I ever did working for my mom; it's the only time my parents will let me leave the house by myself; while I'm at work, I almost feel like I'm a normal kid. During the lunch rush, when cute boys who I remember from elementary school see that I'm working at Hometown Deli and that I've got new boobs, I think they'll have to notice me. After all, I weigh less than a hundred pounds, but my boobs are full Ds. But Ralph is the first man to notice my breasts. I'm not very good with flirting, so I figure it will be good practice to flirt with an older man. Sometimes, Ralph even flirts back. I don't worry about flirting with him because I know he has a wife and two kids and nothing will ever come of it.

One day, Ralph says that it's too slow to keep two girls working and he asks who wants to go home. I want the money, so I ask to stay and my co-worker leaves. When she's gone, I flirt openly with Ralph as he sits near the cash register. As I work around him, I situate my body for his pleasure, arching my back as I reach for extra cups off the top shelves, keeping my legs straight and my ass up when I grab veggies from the bottom shelf of the fridge, squeezing my arms together as I carry heavy packages of meat in front me, pushing my breasts out to make them look bigger, as if that was necessary. We both know what I'm doing and I smile about it until he gets up and pushes me into the back room. Then he grabs me and kisses me. I'm surprised, but I think I kind of like it. But then he kisses me harder and harder and when I try to pull away, he shoves me and I stumble several feet backwards and fall into one of the chairs in the back room.

Ralph starts to undo his belt buckle as he walks toward me in the chair. I get scared. I think about his wife and kids and I think that he'll stop, but he doesn't. When he lowers his pants just far enough to pull out his penis, I really start to panic and I say, "I won't have sex with you!" He can tell that I'm scared because my words come out too high and shrill, like a soft scream. But he keeps walking toward me and I put my hands up to stop him, but he grabs the back of my head and shoves his penis in my mouth. Before I can yell for him to stop and before his penis even gets hard, it's spurting in my mouth and I am gagging. When he's done, he backs away and I run to the sink and wash out my mouth over and over.

Ralph says, "Way to ruin the mood," and pulls up his pants and re-buckles his belt. He walks to the front of the shop and sits down again, as if nothing has happened. I find my leftover cranberry juice from lunch and I drink the rest to try to get rid of the taste, but I can't tell if it makes it better or worse.

I keep working at Hometown Deli because this job is the only good thing I have in a life that I hate. And because I want so badly to be normal, to have money, and to get away from my parents, I don't tell anyone about what happened, except for my best friend, Amanda, and I don't even tell her the real truth. I say, "Ralph and I got it on." She's happy for me. I'm special. I'm special because my breasts are large, larger than Amanda's, larger than any of the other girls' my age. I'm special because these breasts can get an older man, even one who used to be an actor.

But I no longer flirt with Ralph. I get scared that it might happen again, so I don't talk to him unless required by my job. I avoid showing cleavage. I come to work on time and I leave on time.

One day, it starts to snow. The snow won't quit, so Ralph decides to close up shop early and he offers me and his other employee a ride home. I ask her where she lives and it is past where I live, so I think it's safe to get a ride because I know he'll drop me off first. He doesn't. He drives out of the way to her house, even though I become agitated and protest loudly that I should be dropped off first. He makes a ridiculous excuse that doesn't make sense and I don't know what to do. After he drops her off, I sit in the car next to Ralph, rigid and silent, as we drive to my house. Nothing happens.

I've never been so scared in my life.

❧

I meet Mark at Hometown Deli. He's Ralph's age, but I don't think they are anything alike. Mark is very handsome and when I kiss him, I'm not scared. Mark tells me how mature I am for being barely fifteen and how smart I am. He tells me that most other girls my age would never interest him, but I'm special. Mark and I have sex and when the condom breaks, I can tell that he is genuinely worried about me because he goes to the pharmacy right away to buy spermicide.

Mark can't get enough of my big tits and my tight little body, so he offers me a second job at his antique store. My parents agree that I can take on that work if I keep up my grades and my chores and my Bible studies. Working at the antique shop is convenient for fucking because Mark's apartment is connected to it. Sometimes, he bends me over the front counter by the cash register and fucks me from behind among his antiques. Other times, we put up a sign that the shop is closed for lunch and we have sex in his apartment.

One day, Mark takes me into the bathroom for a quickie. He picks me up and sits me on the counter, half on the sink, half not, with the faucet poking into my side. He tears aside my underwear and shoves it in. I keep my shirt on, which I prefer now. Since Ralph, I'm embarrassed of my breasts, how big they are — so big men can't help themselves. Mark fucks me hard, pushes me farther and farther into the corner of the bathroom vanity. It's uncomfortable, painful actually, but I don't say anything because I know by now that it's more important to be sexy than to enjoy it.

I think about how I've never had an "orgasm," or at least I don't think I have. It always seems like the point of sex is to please a man and I think I'm lucky that I'm good at that part of sex at least. And if I'm good at it and if my massive tits can attract older men like Ralph and Mark, then maybe I can attract any older man, preferably a rich one. Maybe I can get a sugar daddy and run away from home, away from the JWs, away from my father who is always watching me.

I call my sister April, who is fourteen years older than me and living in Hawaii, and I tell her about wanting a sugar daddy. I tell her that I want to run away, just like she did. She was sixteen when she disappeared. I was only two years old at the time, so I don't remember her leaving. But I do remember being all alone in the house with my father, while my mother went to work. I remember those long, quiet days punctuated by "naps," when my dad would hold me down so tight I couldn't move and whisper, "go to sleep," over and over, until everything went black.

April asks me if I want to come live with her and her two young sons, instead of running away, and I say yes. She starts negotiating with my parents to let me move to Kihei, Maui, but they aren't convinced. My sister used to be a drunk and a drug addict and they don't know if they can trust her, even though she's been sober for almost two years.

I have sex whenever I get the chance now and I don't think I believe in God anymore. But my parents go to church — or "meetings," as they call it — three times a week and I have no choice but to go with them. I sit next to my best friend, Amanda, during meetings and we scribble little notes to each other on yellow adhesive paper we've expertly placed throughout our Bibles. Amanda and I write about Ralph and Mark. After the meeting, someone picks up my Bible by mistake and turns it over to the elders. I get "disfellowshipped" from the JWs — kicked out of their church — for fornication. When my sister calls again to ask my parents to let me leave, my father is disgusted with me, sick that I've been soiled, tarnished. My mother is hysterical. My parents are glad to get rid of me.

When I move in with April and my nephews, money is very tight, but she's on welfare and she gets food stamps, so we have all the food in the world, all the food I could ever eat, and I can't believe how lucky I am to live with her.

I make new friends easily and I brag to them about how my last boyfriend, Mark, was an older man. Some girls are jealous; other girls just don't get it. I never talk about Ralph, though. I know that it was my fault it happened because I flirted with him, showed off my body to him, teased him with my breasts. I don't want people to know that I could ever be so dumb, so I pretend it never happened.

All the while I'm in high school, my breasts keep growing. I overflow D-cups and buy double-D bras. Then I spill over the tops of those. I call this the "double bubble" because it makes me look like I have four tits. So I yank my bra up and let a bit of my bust fall out the bottom, let the wire cut into the lower section of my breasts, so that it appears that my cleavage is flush with the top of the bra once more.

My sister starts drinking soon after I move to Hawaii, but I don't tell my mom on those rare occasions she calls, because even living with a drunk is better than living with my father. A year later, my sister goes to rehab. When she gets out, my new boyfriend,

Chris, and I move in with her for a few months. We want to save up to leave Hawaii when I graduate from high school in June. Chris and I eventually move to the mainland and settle in Portland. I get a job at a frozen yogurt shop, making $5.75 an hour. I try to focus on my job, on the day-to-day routine of making a living, because when I don't, I start to think about Ralph.

When I think about Ralph, it makes me sick. I think about how dumb it was to flirt with him; how stupid I was for offering to stay at work that day while the other girl — the lucky one — went home; how if I'd been smart, I would've remembered how dangerous grown men can be.

When I think about Ralph, I fill up with hate in my chest, till my breasts feel so full of hate they could overflow, till I think the hate might start to leak from my nipples, so I try to stop it before it starts. I try to shove the memory down.

⤙⤚

Chris gets a job slinging porn at a local porn video rental house. He meets this cool bisexual chick there and thinks we would get along well, so the three of us meet up at a strip club just outside the city. Foxy's Gentlemen's Club doesn't sell alcohol, so the eighteen-to-twenty crowd can see skin too. The added benefit is that girls can go full nude at juice bar-style strip clubs, whereas at alcohol-serving strip clubs, girls have to keep their panties on. I'm barely twenty and have a year till I'm of legal drinking age, so I'm thrilled to be able to see naked women now. I've never had a private dance before, so when I get one from an angelic redhead who smells like amber and vanilla, I'm smitten. Her breasts are small, pouty, perfect things. Breasts that do not induce madness. And because they are safe breasts, I don't have to stare at them; instead I can sink into her eyes, the scent of her skin, the way her hair grazes my face when she gets close.

Chris's friend asks me if I want to go again with her and a week later we're back at Foxy's. This time, as we stare at the beautiful women, she asks, "Doesn't it just make you want to — "

138

I think she's going to say, *fuck 'em?* So I interject an enthusiastic "Yes!"

But instead she says, " — get up there and dance?"

I think, *Well, no, not exactly,* but I say, "Sure," because I don't want to sound lame.

"I'm going to talk to the manager," she says. In five minutes she's back and says, "We start on Monday night!"

I'm scared and nervous, but Foxy's has a good vibe. The girls aren't friendly, but they are sober, since drugs and alcohol are strictly forbidden. Foxy's draws a big audience of guys around my age, some of whom are attractive, or at least not particularly hideous, or at least hygienic.

My very first night working, I walk, trembling and wobbling in my heels, to the first guy I see — a young Mexican boy with a sweet smile — and ask him if he wants a dance. He stares into my eyes the whole song. I swear he doesn't even look at my tits. He keeps saying in his thick Spanish accent, "You are beautiful. You are beautiful. You are beautiful," and I think I have never been so loved as in that moment. I want more. I want to swim in that feeling forever. I'll show off my tits every night of my life just to get it.

I love to strip because the boys and men at the strip club adore me. I always thought having big boobs would finally pay off and I was right. My boobs, which now spill out of triple-D bras, make me *a lot* of money. But it is more than just that: I'm good at stripping and it's better work than customer service, so I quit my day job to spend six or even seven nights a week working at the strip club. The other dancers warm up to me when they realize I'm not going anywhere and when I walk in for my nightly nine p.m. shift, I feel like I've finally found somewhere I belong.

After a year on the pole, I dance with confidence. I stop thinking about the boys in the crowd, the youngest ones, the teens without money who are always clustered closest to the stage. Most of them don't want me or won't admit to it anyway. They're the type to order up a Barbie doll girl, whether they want her or not, just to impress their friends. So when I go on stage, I dance for myself. My song of choice is Rob Dougan's "Clubbed to Death" off the *Matrix* soundtrack that just got released. When I dance to that song, I get lost in my mind and imagine how sexy I am, how every man in the room wishes he could be with me, how even those little boys would kill to get a hold of my big tits and ass. I touch the curves of my body and I imagine myself having sex. If a boy dares to forget his friends and stares at me on stage, I look him right in the eye and imagine we're fucking. He can feel it too.

When I do a private dance for a man, I put my hand on the back of his neck and get real close to his face and look him right in the eye. With my eyes I say, "I love you. I want you. I need you. I have a thirst that only you can quench." Sometimes, he'll forget to look at my tits and close his eyes and I'll get close to his neck and breathe a low, aching moan into his ear.

Then he is mine.

The rush from this domination is the best feeling in the world and I live for these moments. It makes me feel powerful. It makes me feel strong. It makes me feel adored. The rush is the only thing that feels real in my otherwise wasted, wanting life. When I get lost in the dance, I can forget that the love of these men can't compensate for the disgust and contempt I feel for myself. I can forget that their love isn't love.

While I'm drunk on this false sense of security, one of these men becomes my lover. Richard is nineteen, two years younger than me, but is filled with dreams and ideas and spontaneity. I tell him that I have a live-in boyfriend, but that Chris and I have an "understanding" — an open relationship — even though we're about to get married in a few weeks. Richard is devastated.

When Richard tells me he wants me all for himself, I am sure that means this love is real. And when he tells me he can't be with me if I am also with someone else, I end things with Chris three days before our wedding and I get my own apartment. And when he tells me to stop wearing so much black because I look better in pastels, I am not so sure, but I have never been a fashionista, have I? And when he tells me that my friends are annoying, I stop calling them. And when he says he doesn't want to meet my brother when my brother has flown in all the way from the Bay Area to visit me, I assure him he doesn't have to. And when he squeezes my side and says, "There's just a little more to love here," I am hurt, but decide it's ridiculous to get angry about something so small. It *is* ridiculous, *isn't it?* And when he first calls me a bitch, I tell him that will be the last word he ever says to me. I tell him to get out of my apartment and that I need a break. And when I am out one night, fucking a friend who occasionally comes into the club, and Richard calls me over and over and leaves an angry message saying if he finds out I'm out fucking some other guy he'll cut off my pinky toes, I still miss him. And when he shows up at the club one night, I take him back to my house and while we are fucking he says he wants to have a family with me and I say, "Can we talk about this later?" and he asks, "Don't you want to have a family with me?" and I say, "Not right now" and then he comes inside me anyway, which he has never done before. I go to the doctor's the next day and I get the morning-after pill, but apparently it isn't one hndred percent effective.

Richard calls me a whore because of my work. He tells me I would quit stripping if I wasn't such a slut. But even after I quit, he still gets angrier with each day. Scared and without a job, I leave Richard to live with a mutual friend of ours. I am broke and isolated and the most miserable I have ever been in my life. When Richard gets evicted from his apartment a couple months later, he moves in with his friend — *our* friend — and with me. Richard calls me names and he threatens me, but I don't think he'll hurt me under the gaze of our friend. Later, he will prove me wrong.

But before that happens, before he tries to squeeze all breath from my throat, and before I can escape to safety, I find evening office work in the critical care units of a local hospital. One night, the ICU is quiet and a charge nurse comes by my office. We start talking.

I tell her about how I went to live with my crazy sister when I was fifteen.

She tells me how she's taking care of her sister's kids because her sister is a mess too. She says one of her sister's kids is fifteen now, just like I was, and how he has a girlfriend who is everything to him.

She tells me, "He says he doesn't want to live with me, so he's going to marry his girlfriend and they are going to move out together."

I can't stop laughing at the ridiculousness of it.

"Yeah," she says, "but that's teenagers for you."

"Oh man," I say, "kids are so stupid sometimes."

"Well, it's not his fault. He's just a typical teenager."

Then the smile slips off my face and I repeat it: "Kids are so stupid." And for whatever reason, this is the exact moment that it all sinks in. I understand that what Ralph did to me wasn't my fault. I was just a fifteen-year-old kid who didn't know any better and he was an adult who took advantage of me. It wasn't the way I dressed, it wasn't how much cleavage peeked above my shirt, and it wasn't the size of my breasts.

Note: Some names and identifying details have been changed to protect the safety and privacy of the author.

FIFTEEN

Julia Park Tracey

My breasts preceded me
wherever I went
at fifteen;

I knew it,
the newfound keys to some door
that could open up
a wide world
where I was grown-up and liked,
    or not liked;

Boys knew it,
and talked it
and found ways to touch.

My mother knew it,
and warned and scolded
because
    nice girls don't
    nice girls don't
    don't let him go too far

I didn't know
how far was too far
because I was liked
    or not liked
when I went,
and felt so good
    and so bad
when I came back.

Nipples

Fiona Tinwei Lam

I had noticed them before, of course, on my mother, father, women in changing rooms, men at public swimming pools. I'd glance before turning away in embarrassment. They looked like discoloured belly buttons up there on the chest where you weren't supposed to look unless you were rude or a pervert.

But suddenly, when I was around twelve, my nipples started to announce their presence. Before, they'd just seemed like slightly puckered polkadots of tanned skin, or maybe a species of mole. But now they were starting to thicken, becoming — to my horror — more visible, even through my clothes. Puberty was clearly changing everything for the worse.

I was terrified that I'd end up with nipples like my mother's, which were huge dark nubs the colour of liver. (My sister and I had been bottle-fed at my mother's insistence during the heyday of infant formula. My mother, the obstetrician, scoffed at my father, the pediatrician, when he dared to offer a different opinion.) One time when I was eight or nine years old, she proudly squeezed her nipples right in front of me to show me the milk for my baby brother. I already knew that *proper* milk came from cows, was pumped into vats, then cartons, which were shipped to grocery stores, purchased and put in fridges to be poured for a cool, refreshing beverage to accompany cookies. What came from my mother made me think of pus.

In grade six and seven, I tried to push my nipples down and in, hoping they'd go away. They didn't, so I crossed my arms a lot. In grade eight, I wore layers to hide them, as well as the mortifying outlines of the old scratchy ill-fitting bras my mother had dredged up from her ancient stash. First layer, mortifying bra with obtrusive buckles; second layer, undershirt; third, blouse; fourth, T-shirt or cardigan; fifth, raincoat, with lining on cold days, or without on warm days. In the first few months of high school, I'd only take off the coat when seated at my desk in the classroom. In phys. ed., I would reduce the layers and pray we wouldn't go outside in the cold. By the end of grade eight, I had gradually and cautiously settled on three layers, and even that seemed bordering on wanton. All the other girls were wearing jeans and light cotton tops or sweaters, oblivious to what was revealed — perhaps even proud of their natural endowments. I knew enough not to be proud. Pride was dangerous, as proven by the news clippings about rape that my mother left on the pillow on my bed.

Decades later, when I became a mother myself, my nipples had grown into their genetic inheritance. The mantra now was "the breast is best," as chanted by the midwives, doulas, nurses, parenting magazines, lactation consultants, and La Leche League adherents. After I gave birth, so many of these breast experts had scrutinized, grabbed and manipulated my breasts in order to instruct me on the proper latching process, that my self-consciousness withered away.

All that breastfeeding during the first year left my nipples chafed and stinging. I would keep looking down to see if they were bleeding or about to fall off my chest. For two and a half years, I did my duty, praying that my breasts wouldn't become *National Geographic* material. Then much later, I read a *Maclean's* article that stated that breast milk is laden with toxins, especially in the west. One day my kid will accuse me of giving him cancer through misplaced devotion, a fine addition to the list of issues he can discuss with a future therapist.

Note: This creative nonfiction version of *Body Tales* is based on a piece of experimental fiction by the author contained in *ribsauce: a cd/anthology of words by women*, edited by Taien Ng-Chan and published by Véhicule Press.

Bridges

Joelle Barron

When I was a kid, I'd get lost in front of the bathroom mirror, poking at my skin, wondering why I felt no connection between what I saw and who I was. I could see myself touching this *being*, every jab of my finger. But that wasn't me.

As I got older, I'd play with my breasts, too; flick them, watch them jiggle, pinch the nipples until they recoiled and shrank. I understood they were a part of me, but I couldn't cross the vast, blurry gap that seemed to exist between myself and my physical body. I had no bridge; I didn't even have anything for a bridge to cross.

The first time I heard the word "depersonalization" was high up in a psychiatrist's office in downtown Vancouver. "It's a common side effect of trauma," she told me gently. It was a clear day; I looked out the window at the green space far below, and I had the strange sensation that I could just as easily be one of those people down there walking their dogs as I could be myself, sitting up here in this office. The inner fog that separated me from myself lifted briefly, before it deepened again.

I always liked breasts, though I didn't want to; I used to pore over photos of naked people in my dad's form-drawing books and studiously ignored the fact that I found women's bodies just as interesting and exciting as men's. Then I would lie awake at night with my eyes squeezed shut whispering, *I'm not a lesbian, I'm not a lesbian.* I was brought up Catholic, and even though I wasn't totally sure what a lesbian was, I knew I wasn't supposed to be one.

I started taking birth control when I was sixteen, and my breasts quickly went from an A-cup to a B. One day in the high school computer lab, I felt a pleasant weight resting on my forearm. It was a minute before I realized that it was my own breast. I still felt no connection to it, but it was the first time I had actively enjoyed having breasts attached to my body.

I struggled through the first two years of university. I was starting to realize that I didn't feel like a girl. But I didn't feel like a boy, either, and the fact that I could exist outside that binary was still foreign to me. I was deeply in love with a close friend. On my twenty-first birthday, the two of us and another friend got drunk and decided to go skinny dipping at Kitsilano Beach.

It was barely ten at night, and the beach was still crowded with people when we stripped off our clothes and ran screaming into the cool water. The fog around me thickened until everything was silent. I watched my friends from a distance, how beautiful they looked, how they seemed to *belong* in their bodies. I felt something that I don't have a word for; a combination of deep love for my friends, and an even deeper desire to be able to leave my body and cease to exist.

In grad school, aware of clichés, I experimented with hallucinogens. The first time I took LSD, I couldn't believe how small I felt. "I'm so small!" I kept saying to my friend. "Why do I feel so small?"

"You are small," he told me. I realized that it wasn't that I felt small; I felt grounded. I was feeling, for the first time in my life, what it felt like to inhabit my own body. Later, in the shower, I touched my breasts. I wondered how I'd feel if I woke up one day and they weren't there. I decided I wouldn't mind at all.

Then I got pregnant.

My pregnancy was difficult. I was sick for the first four months; I lost fifteen pounds and lived on soda crackers. Motherhood is viewed as the epitome of womanhood. The idea of giving birth made me nervous, not because I feared pain or embarrassment, but because I disliked the idea of a room full of strangers looking at my body in varying degrees of nudity and seeing it as a *woman's* body.

As I began to show, I felt more and more uncomfortable with my inability to escape from my womanhood. Before my pregnancy, I could use the way I dressed and wore my hair as a physical representation of the distance I felt from society's interpretations of what makes a woman. With my pregnant belly, I felt that my gender identity, and my sexuality, were too readily presumable. I wanted to hide from my body as I always had before, but there was nowhere to go. The fetus growing inside of me kept me firmly attached to myself — or at least to my body — in a way I had never experienced.

My feelings about my breasts went from ambivalence to fascination. Within the first month, my pale pink nipples had turned dark brown, easier to spot with bleary, newborn eyes. I was five months along the first time I squeezed my nipple in the tub and watched pus-like colostrum drip into the water and slick on the surface like oil.

Rather than inhabiting my body, I began to feel as though I was inhabiting my breasts. It was comforting to lie in the tub and imagine being tucked away among the fatty tissue, pressure of a hard rib bone against my back, and a sound like water rushing through pipes as my body prepared to make the food that would nourish my child for her first months and years of life.

My labour and birth didn't go the way I wanted or expected, and I ended up having a Caesarean section. I didn't get to hold my baby until over an hour after she was born. When I did finally have her in my arms, I started nursing her right away. I had the overwhelming sense that love wasn't what I had thought it was before.

For the first months of her life, for all intents and purposes, my daughter and I were one. She nursed every hour; my nipples cracked and bled. This sense of oneness was different than those ten months we were bound by the umbilical cord. Then, our attachment felt tolerably oppressive, like a tight turtleneck. After she was born, my breasts were our point of connection, the bridge between her body and mine. Always an afterthought, now they were everything; alive and unpredictable, how they could be rock hard one second and deflated the next. The unfamiliar stinging tingle of let-down, the velocity of pressurized milk, sudden realization that all my T-shirts were ruined.

Once, when she was a couple of months old, I looked into my daughter's eyes while she was nursing, and I realized that there was a person looking back at me. It was the first time I had seen the light of recognition come over her. She flailed her little hand up to my cheek. I felt as if I was meeting her, again, for the first time.

I've felt everything about my body, from ambivalence, to loathing, to love. But I've never felt that it was *necessary*. Having a child made me grateful my body exists as it does, even if I still feel no connection to it. As my daughter grows, sits, crawls, walks, she becomes more and more aware that she is her own person, separate from me. Other people can feed her and comfort her. But my breasts are still our connection, and I believe that even when she's done with them, that connection will persist.

My breasts are my bridge to her. That bridge brings me closer, somehow, to myself.

Taxi

Miranda Pearson

In a taxi bowling down the
wide boulevards of Berlin, how he

touched me, my black dress cut low —
back then we didn't know —

    (No, rot is wrong,
    that's what nectarines do.

    This *is* me, I grew it
    in this hothouse gone askew).

Think of the gasping blind lovers
who fell, who unlaced, who

looked   unhooked,
    who —

men's eyes —
they could not see

beneath the white veneer
to the spider's nest within.

    The doctor said
    this has been growing in you for about ten years —

a spoonful. A *soupcon.*
We all carry it, the seed of our departure.

A letter. With instructions —
though you may not yet decipher them.

Kept close. Sealed.

OPENING AND CLOSING

Allison Jane Smith

There was a lump in my breast.

It had been there for three years. Sometimes it was bigger and sometimes it was smaller, changing with the amount of estrogen in my body, like tides change with the moon. Aren't our bodies supposed to be sensitive to the lunar cycle? Maybe the lump changed with the moon, too.

Three years earlier, a doctor had said it was benign and would disappear, but it was still there. Three years was enough time to make me feel a slight ripple of unease.

I sat in a paper dressing gown, feet swinging from the examination table, and wondered if this would be what brought me back to Canada. Would I be one of those expats who lived abroad until they got pregnant or fell ill and then returned, medical card in hand, to get treatment?

The lump was one item on a list of things to get checked out before returning to Cambodia. I needed an x-ray for a knee injured in a motorbike accident, a stool test to check for a parasite common in Southeast Asia, a blood test to see if I was iron deficient. Where I lived in northwestern Cambodia, there was no guarantee an x-ray would be read correctly or an iron deficiency would be properly identified. It was better to do the tests while visiting my parents in Manitoba.

The examination room was white and clean. A poster showing a wide, green lawn warned chemical pesticides can cause cancer, particularly in children.

The doctor, a woman, conducted the breast exam cautiously, careful to feel my breasts under the gown but not to look at them. She was from South Africa, and I wondered if her discretion had been learned since arriving in my parents' small, rural town, with its shame and prudishness, or if she had brought it with her from Africa.

Impatient with her tentativeness, I moved the gown from my chest to show her the lump. It was large enough to be visible, making the skin on the surface of my breast pucker in strange ways. I hated seeing it when I looked in the mirror.

The doctor announced there also was a cyst in the right breast. I frowned. I had come for a second opinion on the lump in my left breast, not to hear about growths in the right one.

This wasn't the first I had heard of a cyst in my right breast, though it was the first I had taken it seriously. Before I had left Cambodia a week earlier, a friend had told me there was a lump in my right breast. When he said this, I had clutched my chest, searching for it. Feeling nothing, I dismissed the comment.

Yet here was this doctor, saying there was a benign cyst in the right breast as well. My friend — that was the noun we used, our brief entanglement before my departure notwithstanding — had been right.

The lump in my left breast was much larger, however. Despite what I had been told before, this doctor said it may never get smaller and it may never disappear. I needed to decide if I wanted it removed.

"It's probably a fibroid," she said in her lilting South African accent, "but if you'd like to have another ultrasound or biopsy to confirm that, we can do it, it's no problem."

I had nearly passed out at the first biopsy because of my intense fear of needles, which the experience had done nothing to assuage. Feeling a needle pierce my chest to take something from it had been invasive and horrifying. I felt queasy remembering the procedure, a worried nurse flitting around the table, placing a cold cloth on my forehead, trying to keep me conscious.

Instead, I asked for a second ultrasound, not because I wanted to confirm the diagnosis, but because I wanted to stall for time to consider whether I wanted surgery. I couldn't make the decision right then and there, sitting half-naked in a tiny examination room beside posters screaming *think of the children!*

After the appointment, I got bloodwork done. I turned away as the needle entered my arm.

A few days later, a friend and I went to a Mary Pratt exhibition. Her paintings were overwhelmingly still lifes of domestic scenes, and they were beautiful. Jars of jam sparkled like precious stones and tin foil shone like silver jewellery underneath pale cuts of fish.

Many of the paintings were of food, chopped and divided. Split pomegranates, broken eggshells, filleted fish, a piece of cake.

Some of the paintings were unexpectedly affecting. The pomegranates spilled red juice across foil, and the broken eggshells were hollow and desperate. Both paintings were lonely.

The commentary accompanying the exhibition explained how Pratt's paintings reflected what women do: they wrap things up and they cut them open, just as their bodies are subject to episodic opening, from intercourse to childbirth.

We open, we close. I imagined my breast, split open for the lump to be removed. A scalpel cutting through skin above my heart, someone reaching to remove tissue, and then sewing me shut again. I shuddered.

That evening, Katie and I went to a bar. We ordered poutine, because real poutine was not available in Cambodia, and living there had made me crave things I rarely wanted before I couldn't have them.

The poutine was complemented by the free shots some guys bought for the entire bar. The tequila burned on the way down. Katie passed me her cider as a chaser.

Lubricated by the alcohol, we spent the evening talking about places we had been, people we had known in university, sex we were and weren't having. I didn't mention the lump, because I had decided not to have it removed.

My certainty disappeared only days later, as I waited for the hospital to call to make an ultrasound appointment. Did I want the lump gone?

I considered how much bother I was willing to go to to have my breast "normal" again, to return it to a smooth, feminine state. I was twenty-five years old and my breasts were supposed to be flawless. Was it vanity to consider returning to this ideal? Though at times the lump caused me mild discomfort, it was a stretch to say it was painful. Did that mean I was considering cosmetic surgery?

I hadn't thought I was someone who would consider cosmetic surgery. Cosmetic surgery was for superficial middle-aged house-wives concerned about laugh lines, or for tragic, unfortunate burn victims wanting to look normal again. It wasn't for young, healthy women like me.

I considered polling men for their opinions. How unattractive was a breast with a lump? The men I had been involved with over the past three years had had different opinions, from one who had dismissively said no man would even notice, to my friend who had immediately noticed and then mostly avoided my left breast in favour of the right.

I felt slightly ashamed for caring about what men thought. I was supposed to make decisions about my body for me, not for others. The only opinion that mattered was mine. Right?

By the time the hospital called, it was too late. They wanted to set the appointment for the following week, by which time I would have already left for another part of Canada.

"It's fine, I don't need the appointment."

The receptionist was nervous at my carelessness. "If it's something that needs to be checked out..."

"No, really, it's fine."

She reluctantly let me end the call. I knew she went home that evening to tell her husband she had spoken to a woman who was in denial about the reality of finding a lump in her breast.

Some people just don't take their health seriously, Jake, I imagined her saying as she spooned mashed potatoes onto their four-year-old daughter's plate. *She thinks she's immune to cancer.*

After a month in Canada, I returned to Cambodia. Over a year earlier, after a three-week visit to Cambodia, I had moved to Asia on a whim. Though I had scarcely given a thought to relocating to another continent, I couldn't stop thinking about the lump. It wanted to be noticed; it swelled before my period, before retreating below the surface of my breast to wait for another surge of estrogen.

My work, my friends, and my life were in Cambodia, and I had no reason to return to Canada anytime soon. Having the surgery in Canada would require sitting on a waiting list for months, and I didn't have months to spare. If I wanted to have the lump removed, it would be in Thailand, the haven of medical tourists from around the world.

Two months after returning to Cambodia, my visa expired, requiring me to leave the country and re-enter. I decided to take the opportunity to assess my options for having surgery in Bangkok.

After I booked the appointment, I had a dream I was at the clinic. It turned into a nightmare when the doctors told me I needed another biopsy.

I panicked and left the clinic. I couldn't go through that again, I just couldn't.

The hospital in Bangkok was one of the best in the world. People came from far and wide to visit. The signs were in Thai, English, Arabic and Chinese, and the waiting rooms were as multicultural as gates at the airport.

There was a Starbucks next to the patient reception desk, and chic paintings hung in the waiting rooms. My patient number and birthdate had been automatically configured as my own personal username and password for the Wi-Fi. I sent emails and chatted with a friend on Facebook as I waited for my appointment.

I was called in and lay on the table beside the ultrasound machine. The technician asked me to open my gown, leaving me uncovered except for a pair of lacy black panties, which seemed wholly inappropriate for the situation. I felt vulnerable as I lay there, exposed from neck to groin.

The technician asked about the previous biopsy as she spread cold gel on my chest. I cringed from the sensation and explained the biopsy had shown the lump was a benign fibroid. It wasn't cancer; I didn't need a biopsy to see if it was cancer.

They examined not only my left breast but also the right one, making me tenser. Would they make me have a biopsy for that cyst? Please God, not another biopsy.

I changed back into my clothes and waited for the consultation with the surgeon, still worrying about the chance that I would need another biopsy. My phobia made it more important to avoid a needle than receive an accurate diagnosis, and while I knew how silly that was, I couldn't change it.

The surgeon was a squat Thai woman with impeccable English and a last name too long for me to attempt pronouncing. Her quiet competence immediately appealed to me, and I relaxed just a little bit, even though it was intimidating to be meeting with her by myself, far away from home.

Like the ultrasound technician, she wanted to hear more about the biopsy. "Was it a little needle or a big needle?" she asked.

I didn't say I had been too busy trying not to hyperventilate to look at it. But I remembered the feeling of the needle in my breast, its conspicuous presence so different from the quick pinch of a needle in the arm. "It seemed pretty big to me," I said.

She laughed and mimicked the puncturing sound the needle had made. "Did it sound like that?"

"Yes!" I said. "It sounded like something had punched me! Well, not punched me, but..."

She nodded. "It was the one-point-five millimetre, then."

One-point-five millimetres? Something one and a half millimetres wide was capable of causing me nightmares? I was pathetic.

The surgeon carried on. "Most fibroids like the one in your breast, 80 percent in fact, are between two to three centimetres. Yours is four centimetres, bigger than most.

"The size means it could be a fibroid, or it may be a different kind of tumour that could turn malignant. The only way to know is to test it after removing it surgically."

Malignant. This was the first the word had been uttered in my presence, and I didn't like hearing it.

Suddenly warm, I tried to think: What were the questions I should ask about the diagnosis? What did I need to know to get my insurance company to pay for the surgery?

If someone else were with me, they would know what to ask.

I had taken a friend with me to my appointments in Canada. We had watched the news while waiting for the mammogram, a flat-screen television broadcasting Jack Layton into the waiting room. As it happened, that had been the day Jack Layton had announced he had cancer. We had joked darkly that everyone did.

There was no one here to joke with.

I felt small and foolish. Why hadn't I thought about this part?

The doctor explained the procedure, which would require placing me under a general anesthetic. I would need to stay in the hospital for four to six hours after the surgery. I realized that when I woke up, it would be a Thai nurse who greeted me, rather than anyone I knew.

I took the medical certificate declaring I needed surgery and an estimate of the cost to present to my insurance company. I didn't know what I would do if they refused to pay. I would think about that later.

Dazed, I left the clinic, passing through its glass atrium to the damp city outside. The humidity was as dense as my thoughts as I wandered, looking for a place to get a drink.

Instead, I came across an ornate Catholic church and went inside. After a day of focusing on my body, it seemed fitting to take time to consider my spirit.

I had arrived during a mass. Desperate to take communion, I slid into a pew, kneeling and crossing myself at the appropriate times.

During the homily, the priest spoke about sacrificing for Jesus. I wasn't interested in sacrifice; I would have preferred to hear about comfort.

My mind wandered as I thought of the conversation I needed to have with the insurance company, the work I needed to get done the next day, the way I wished I had thought to bring someone with me to Bangkok. I thought of the men I had dated and wished I were going home to a bed where someone familiar was waiting, rather than to a hostel with a twin bed and white sheets.

The church congregation was as multicultural as the hospital patients had been. Black, white, Asian, we all lined up for communion to receive the blood and body of the Lamb. When I reached the front of the line, I was disappointed to find that while bread was on offer, there was no wine.

I ducked out of the service early and found a cafe. After a cold pomegranate tea, I ordered a glass of wine. "White?" the server asked.

I shook my head. "Red."

It was served in a cheap glass. As I sipped it, I considered again my motivation for having the lump removed from my breast. I had gone from rejecting a second ultrasound in Canada to undergoing a lumpectomy in Thailand, in the name of — what? Vanity? Femininity? Peace of mind? I thought of the many things breasts represent, and I thought too of pomegranates, split open and seeping blood onto the table, and broken eggshells, hollow and lonely.

We're women; we open and we close. Our bodies expand and contract, sometimes of our own will, and sometimes not.

Skin Deep

Devin Casey

I wouldn't be talking about my breasts if they were still here, but they aren't. I'm transgendered, and in 2014 I had top surgery: a double mastectomy with nipple grafts and remodelling. Trans is not binary, it's a spectrum and it's fluid. Not everything applies to every body, but for some boobs are a signifier: you really want them, or you really want them gone. Others have them, enjoy them, and decide they're worth keeping.

At age nine, my breasts started developing. It was a shock. "What's this? What the hell? I never asked for these..." From when I was really little I realized I was trans, but didn't have a word for it. I was attracted to girls, so I just thought I was gay. It was really disappointing when my breasts started to develop. How do you postpone the inevitable?

I was one of the first in my class to get boobs. It was horrible. By grade seven, I had some serious tits. In the seventies, bras lifted and separated, and although I never wore low-cut shirts or anything, there was no hiding my breasts. Clothes never fit me.

My mom has big breasts as well, although none of her sisters do. The two of us just ended up in the line for two double scoops!

The first person who said anything about my breasts to my face was Sean, who would eventually be my best friend, for life. It was grade seven, my second day at Catholic school. Sean was sitting behind me, on my right-hand side. He whispered in my ear, but loud enough for people to hear, "Oh my god, you have giiii-annnnt tits." I stood up, put my hands on my hips, and loudly told him to "drop dead," a remark that's haunted me since. I was immediately banished to the hallway. Then I heard, "Get the fuck out of my classroom," and Mr. Babarad ejected Sean more violently, throwing a garbage can and breaking his own Rolex. That moment showed me how disruptive breasts could be. Sean and I bonded in the hallway.

When we were fourteen, Sean and I used to go to a theatre in the east end of Toronto to see *The Rocky Horror Picture Show*. Our gay lives hadn't really taken off yet, but we loved the outlaw sexuality, and the movie was a real revelation to me, particularly the nipple shot because Columbia was not perfect. Boobs didn't have to be identical twins. Or was it really a shadow?

For most of my life, my breasts got all the attention because they were so big. Guys would talk to my tits and not talk to me, or they'd make stupid jokes, thinking they were being original. "Hey! Jump up and down!" Those breasts were objects of ridicule, pieces of my body that I never wanted and didn't ask for. They would walk into the room before I did.

As a teenager, I was a waitress and I can't tell you the number of times I dipped my right boob into things on my trays. Businessmen would make rude, condescending comments: offering to lick the sauce off my shirt, and worse. As if giving me a tip would make up for the degrading remarks.

I've spent thousands of dollars on bras, good bras, not just sports bras that crush your boobs into your spine and push them out your backside. Seventies and eighties bras were "RAM tough, built to last." The only thing that would give out was the clasp: when they made elastic they really made elastic.

Running was a nightmare. I played soccer in high school and I did run then, but only because I wanted the fucking ball and you weren't going to get it off me. I have to really want something in order to run.

I never would shower at school and would change in the bathroom. I wouldn't get naked in front of other girls because it was embarrassing and uncomfortable. I knew I was gay but I didn't want anyone to call me on it so I'd avert my eyes. I'm an expert on shoes because I looked at so many!

Having sex, I would take my shirt off but often would leave my bra on, just for safety purposes. Flailing 38Es can inflict quite a bit of damage, including a black eye or two! Over the years, my girlfriends were envious, and that was all fine and dandy unless they wanted to touch them. Sometimes it was a drag to be bigger than the girl I was feeling up. When I met a woman with breasts as large as mine, they were very enjoyable, but I felt her pain…

Every summer, at the Michigan Womyn's Music Festival, women would be walking around naked, topless, packing… every version and every shade of skin was there (except for the trans girls who were stopped at the gate and made to feel very unwelcome). It was lovely, but you wouldn't catch me naked except for standing in the dreaded shower line. I would look around then and think, life isn't so bad after all: bodies are just bodies. Otherwise, I wouldn't take off my top; I would just roast.

I knew I was different then, but I didn't consider myself trans. I was still trying to navigate the lesbian world, which was confusing too. I'd been out for so long, it was odd that there was still something missing. I was definitely on the butch side, but I had big boobs and long, curly hair, so my identity wasn't clear cut, and I never labelled myself anyway. David Bowie's recent death has made me think back to that time: he was the first person to publicly transform himself. Sure, it was from a guy to a girl, and back again, but still… he was gender-fluid and that's okay. But at this time in my life, that isn't me.

When I was growing up, we didn't have air conditioning, so sometimes my mom and I would hang out by the open fridge and bond over our boob sweat. She was sympathetic about the pain of having big breasts. She'd get sores under hers. That wasn't a problem for me until I started working at manual labour, landscaping and doing major physical work outside. It would start off like a rash and the salty sweat would burn like hellfire. My bra would get wet and then if I had to put it back on, that was really painful, and also gross.

Mom would say she wished she could just chop hers off. She'd point to them and pretend to fire a gun — pow! pow! giggle! I'd think, I wish it was that easy. And for that moment, I would mean it, but I don't think she did! This was the first honest conversation we had about it: in the late seventies and early eighties. That was the first time I thought of that: I must have been transitioning in my head for a long time.

Mom would take her shirt off when we were out fishing sometimes. She liked to be wild and free. She's a hot-looking woman and likes to go topless, but I never felt comfortable with that. I never identified with the twins, so why would I want to do that? I have always liked my body, though. If you're talking about a killer figure, I had one. When I was young, I had a terrific body. It just had extra parts that I didn't want.

My back really started to hurt when I did landscaping but I was strong and I could adjust myself. I started having chiropractic adjustments in high school but my breasts always seemed to be in the way. I'd roll over in bed and catch my nipple and it hurt. When I got my period, my breasts were heavier and excruciating. You know that feeling right before they blow up? Any extra weight went to my tits first, and the fatter I got, the bigger my boobs got. They were a lot of work for no reason. They were just there. I never wanted children, so they had no purpose. And they floated: I discovered that in a hot tub. Sean had always called them "flotation devices," but imagine my surprise when I found out he was right.

Don't get me wrong, though, I do like breasts. Just on other people.

In my early forties, I came back home when Sean was dying, and reconnected with an old friend who'd transitioned. I hadn't really thought about transitioning before, but I started thinking seriously about it then. I'd spent the first fifty years of my life in a woman's body, so why not spend the next fifty as a man and really be myself, grasping the whole human experience?

I knew about androgyny, of course, but figured that if I was starting from scratch, I could reinvent myself. My family was accepting. I'm lucky as hell: they were used to me as gay — I broke them in at a young age — and now they accept me as trans. Talk about coming out twice. We're pretty close, and I came out to my aunts and uncles first, and then my mom. She had been in a relationship with a really judgmental man and she didn't need the added crap, not from me.

Once I started transitioning, I never bound my breasts. I knew binding was unhealthy. I'd seen it first-hand and was taken aback by how painful it looked. People who bind make that choice, and I can understand that sometimes it's the safest choice, but I wish there was another way. Society just doesn't let us go there.

I wanted surgery but didn't think it was financially possible. Then I had a windfall and decided instead of taking the trip of a lifetime, I would take a trip that would last a lifetime. I decided to do something for myself.

I didn't go through CAMH, which was the only government-funded gender reassignment program, because of the enormous lineup and the three-year wait for surgery. Someone else decides if you deserve to transition or not. It puts you directly in harm's way for the waiting period because you're living between genders and that's dangerous for everyone. I thought, Fuck that! I've lived like this my whole life. Having to travel to a CAMH surgeon in Quebec was ridiculous, so I found a wonderful surgeon here in Ontario who had done work on some of my friends. At my first appointment, I was stoked, excited. I felt like I'd been let inside Santa's workshop. I wasn't going for a facelift, I was going for a life lift. It was amazing. I was totally comfortable. It was a liberating experience.

I had absolutely no second thoughts. You try living for forty years with a sore back and boob sweat. I'm fifty-three, and just thinking back to all that now makes my back hurt.

The day of my surgery, I was nervous and knew it would be painful, but I also knew that the pain and the discomfort would never equal what I'd already suffered. One guy said it was the most painful thing he'd ever gone through. I disagree! In my opinion, I've had heartbreak that was worse!

I joked with the doctor that I wanted to know how much they weighed. I bet they were the equivalent of a six-pack of beer. When I came out of surgery, I saw they'd written down the weight on my hand because I was too fucked-up to remember the numbers. I got some tall boys from the beer store and weighed them: my breasts had weighed the equivalent of two tall boys each. That's nearly 1.5 kilos or five pounds, half a glass less than a six-pack.

The day after surgery, when I was changing my dressings, I looked in the mirror and said, "Yup, they really are gone!" It was an odd sensation. I felt taller but I had a different centre of gravity and I had trouble balancing. I still sit too far away from the dinner table sometimes because I forget that I can sit closer.

Dr. Hugh Maclean and his team did an absolutely amazing job. After my bandages were unwrapped, it was like Rocky dancing with Frankenfurter. My nipple grafter was very skilled: hot, funny and smart. She'd warned me that I might lose sensation in my nipples, but I can feel everything and my scars have healed well. Even though I've been taking testosterone for six years, my skin has stayed very elastic and soft. I must have good genes or something, but it's made a difference.

My life without breasts has been magnificent. My back doesn't go out. Running has never been fun for me, although now I could if I wanted to. I'm only sorry I couldn't donate those boobs to a boobie bank for trans girls who want them!

I rarely went swimming before surgery, even though I like it, and the first time I swam after surgery was the first time I'd taken my shirt off in public. My girlfriend and I were alone in the pool, but it still felt funny and floating was definitely different: I almost sank! But on Pride, I walked down the street with my shirt open, and it felt great.

A few months ago, I was under a sink, fixing pipes, when I got a reminder call about a mammogram. I started laughing hysterically, and the poor girl on the phone had no idea why. I said, "I don't think I'll be needing one of those again." She asked if I was sure. I looked down, and assured her that I was! Unfortunately, I can't escape Pap smears…

Since surgery, I feel more handsome than I ever considered myself to be pretty. It's a new era. It's so liberating. It was a revelation, wearing clothes that actually fit me.

Even if you're thinking about transitioning as an older person, do it! It's worth it!

A lot of trans people out there choose not to have surgery, but it was the right decision for me and I'm grateful that I could pay for it myself and do it the way I wanted to.

I understand people who need to find ways to fund their transition and I would never judge anyone for the choices they make: cooperating with CAMH, using GoFundMe, or earning the money through prostitution. If you've already made the dangerous decision to turn tricks to pay for your surgery, for god's sake take steps to be as safe as you can. Keep your boobie dream alive.

It's been pretty positive for me, but there is blowback and fall-out when you're transitioning. It can be a crappy experience and sometimes you forget how other people see you. For a couple of years when I was transitioning, I had facial hair and breasts. I'd make sure to wear layers of loose shirts and usually a leather jacket. One hot day, I made a mistake and took off two layers and walked down an alley to the store wearing just a T-shirt and jeans. Coming back onto the sidewalk, a guy crossed the street toward me, making an exploding head gesture and yelling, "What the fuck are you?" I thought, what awaits? A violent beating? Death? Cause it's not going to be a conversation. Yet again, my boobs had put me in danger.

Sometimes now, I forget my boobs are gone and I'm just myself, and I call a straight guy "Hon." I caught myself doing that with an electrician at work the other day and grinned to myself thinking, hmmm, does that make me totally gay? I'm okay with that!

Now, I'm just another guy on the street. And that means you can go brim to brim with somebody and they aren't going to back off because they realize you're a girl, which has happened. That dynamic is gone. Now, I just go, "Look bud, it's okay…" and I back off.

Before I had my surgery, my girlfriend said, "Your body is going to feel different and I'm not sure how I'm going to feel about that."

I said, "I can hug you closer."

I feel deep gratitude for my life now. I'm privileged and I get that, although I've worked hard for some of it. I've had such an easy transition, not as glamorous as Caitlyn's but not harrowing. I have a job at a non-profit social service organization that allows me safe passage in my daily existence. I've lost friends but my family is still there for me. Some friends have outed me to make themselves seem cool for knowing a trans person, others have betrayed me by outing me to ex-girlfriends who didn't know and didn't need to. Ex-girlfriends have said they didn't know that was even on my radar. People can be cruel. But I've kept friends too, and made new ones. If you're going to define me by your perception of my body, I don't need you in my life.

If you know someone who is transitioning, stand up for them, but don't out them to make yourself seem better. It's easy to misunderstand: friends do it. Strangers do it. There's a lot of prejudice and intolerance and trans people deal with it all on a daily basis. I can understand why people go away to transition. Being in between is not easy. But now I'm out the other side. I'm now more fully myself, with gratitude for what I was, but also for what's to come. A weight was lifted off my chest and I can move forward.

Some of that weight was just flesh, but it goes deeper than that. In the grand scheme of things, we all want to be accepted, in our bodies, by the people we love and want to spend time with.

I wanted to end this with something profound, but really, this isn't an ending. It's a new beginning for all of us. As more people embrace their trans identity, society will transition too. And to those girls who are still girls, and still have their girls, please look after your boobs. That goes for you, too, gentlemen who still have your girls!

The Balloon Stuffer

Sadie Johansen

The story of my breasts starts sometime around the age of four or five, seventeen years before I finally have them. I can remember very clearly playing hide-and-seek with my brother when my favourite hiding spot was my mother's closet. I would hide behind her dresses wishing someday I could wear anything as beautiful and have it fit! At the time all I could do was play dress-up and stuff the dresses with balloons or socks. It was fun, but saddening knowing I would never have my own. It wasn't until much later in life I learnt what hormone replacement therapy could do. So I wished at every birthday and with every snow angel. I prayed at every chance that some higher power would give me the breasts and body my mind knew I was supposed to have.

This deep sadness, combined with my fervent wishing, persisted until after puberty when I started trying to hide, even from myself. It was a very painful time having these male changes forced upon me. I was still afraid of swimming because it meant showing my bare, flat and hairy chest to the world but I refused to accept why. The simple act of looking at myself in the mirror sent me into spirals of depression. Why did my body look like this? Why wasn't I growing breasts? It felt as though my own body was betraying me but I refused to accept the truth that I was trans.

In the summer of 2008, something happened that turned my life upside down and would eventually lead to me getting my breasts. I was at a nudist beach on a small lake located on Cortes Island at night when nobody else was around to see my body, or so I thought. I took nearly a week working up courage to go. A beautiful, young brown-eyed woman wearing a long flowing skirt and her wonderfully tattooed friend came walking up the beach while I was freaking out at the sight of other people and the thought of them seeing my boobless, male-looking body. Somehow, even with

168

my mind screaming in anxiety, the woman and I became great friends and, later each other's first loves. After three years together, she knew me better than I knew myself and eventually helped me accept who I am. Her words helped me, as well as her love, and I slowly realized that as much as I loved her, I also needed to have a feminine body for my mind to be at peace. I didn't handle it well at the time but looking back I am very thankful for my time with her, even though it eventually went up in flames largely because of my inability to accept myself.

Almost a year after my relationship with the girl with a long flowing skirt and after much self-reflection and time alone, I started hormone replacement therapy. The first few months were some of the happiest times of my life. The changes were slow, very slow. But I knew they were coming and progress was happening. Every night I would feel my chest getting a little softer, my areolas and nipples becoming bigger. I couldn't help but grin from ear to ear that I finally had the beginning of my boobs. I had waited so long and made so many wishes. They were almost non-existent in size but I was exceptionally happy to have any boobs at all.

It wasn't until about a year into hormone replacement therapy that my breasts really became noticeable. It was a very sudden and shocking but wonderful change. I kept bumping them into doorways and shelves only to scream out in my pain from my sensitive, growing nipples. I learnt fairly fast to give them more room. Two years into my transition, my breasts are still slowly growing and will do so for at least another three years when they will be at the point of growth that most women my age are. But it doesn't matter to me. I love my breasts, whatever the size. I can wear the dresses I always wanted to, without balloons stuffed into them. I can look in the mirror and see myself and be happy.

Amazon

Betsy Struthers

Hope for a clear road: no tanker trucks, no
driver with "I only brake for Jesus"
on the bumper of her van,

no glaring sun or snow squalls either, no
black ice to whisk the wheels right out
from under, spin you out of control

like a runaway train, you said, the days
careening from callback to biopsy,
diagnosis to surgery. You wake

in the recovery room, look down
at the sheet concave on half your chest —

just last night you were out dancing,
"demolition site" lipsticked
on the swell of your troubled breast.

Reclaiming My Thorns

Maggie Wojtarowicz

In 1990, my favourite band, Depeche Mode, released *Violator*. The album cover featured a slender rose that would become symbolic of my life's journey; a journey that I began to share years later with an email update, which I called "New Thorns on My Roses," when I was diagnosed with breast cancer. Back in 1990, though, I had other things on my mind.

That year, at age sixteen, like most of my classmates, I was learning to drive and suffering peer pressure to conform. I alone, though, was also being diagnosed with dystonia: a neurological condition that was expected to affect my movements and speech for the rest of my life. Mine was an "early onset" diagnosis, further marking me unusual in my unusualness. I began to quickly discover how painful dystonia can be, but I knew that it usually is not life-threatening. By my twenties and thirties, I understood how distracting and disconcerting it can be to someone who doesn't know why I move and sound the way I do. When I speak, the muscles in my face and neck tighten, pulling my neck sideways and back, and the tenseness gripping my throat makes me fight against my body to squeeze out my words coherently. When I am still, my limbs twitch; when I smile, my lips twist into a grimace; when I do a shoulder check while riding my bike, pain shoots down my back and pedestrians assume I'm making faces at them. Although all this is unintentional, it is very much visible, and therein lay my biggest challenge with it.

Then, at age thirty-six, I found a lone, rice-grain-sized hard mass in my left breast. Unlike with my previous lumps, which the doctors had deemed benign, this time, I was shocked. Six weeks of ultrasounds, "just in case" mammograms of both breasts, and several needle biopsies confirmed even more tumours in my right breast, all of them cancerous. For diagnoses as aggressive as mine, the Cancer Agency urges doctors to prescribe the full range of treatments: surgeries, various chemotherapies, radiation treatments, hormone therapies, and where genetic testing indicates, the removal of both ovaries. Even if I embraced them all, these invasive treatments could not guarantee saving my life or preventing a recurrence.

It was a sunny Vancouver April day, with cherry blossoms and rosebuds in bloom, when I found myself sitting in my surgeon's bare office that was adorned only by a small window over the examination table. With my file in hand, my surgeon swooshed into the room, gave her best attempt at an acknowledging smile, dove her hand into the metal cabinet beneath me to retrieve a packet, and then settled on her stool in front of me. Unceremoniously, she handed me my copy of the breast cancer kit. I would find reference materials for all the stages of treatment, she explained, and an organizer to keep track of my appointments and symptoms. I found myself dumbfounded at her matter-of-factness when in one breath she covered the contents of the resource kit, the results in my file, and her recommendation that I agree to the removal of both breasts. "This," she said, "will give you the best chances of recovery without recurrence given your age and how much your cancer has already spread." Strangely, I felt grateful that she delivered it all without betraying emotion; it made it easier for both of us to focus on the facts.

Once I left my surgeon's office, my emotions caught up with the facts. I went out onto the lawn in front of the medical building, and for the first time in years, I cried. I sat down and watched through my tears as the deafening stream of cars whizzed by on the busy thoroughfare. I could not face getting onto my bike and riding home just yet. There was no one I wanted to call. There was not even a bench for me to lean on. I sat on the patch of grass, feeling grateful this once for the privacy afforded by the four tonnes of metal armour around the people zooming past me.

Sitting there outside that dispassionate medical building, I reflected on the mixed relationship I've had with my breasts. *Sure, you've mostly been a disappointment, but you're still mine!* My thoughts rebelled. *So much has been taken from me, and now you too?*

Like most people, having breasts lent me a good part of my female identity — but that was complicated by having always had small breasts and a tall, boyish figure. The near invisibility of my breasts had been traumatizing, particularly in my formative years when other unwanted and devastating changes were also gripping my body. I had so often been mistaken for a boy as a teen. Other kids, boys, imposed this false identity on me, and it eroded my self-image as a woman.

My grief then shifted to ruminations about how over the years, the effects of my dystonia had severely undermined my overall self-identity as well. Although I'd learned to trust that dystonia did not affect my intellect or my ability to enjoy life, I found that living with it can seriously wear on self-esteem and the desire to persevere. It has been incredibly difficult for me to be continually remarked upon in public and misjudged in job interviews. Shifting my gaze from the fast-moving traffic to the slug making its way across the lawn, I pondered the difference. *Other things don't seem that bad when you have dystonia! The worst thing that cancer can do is kill me, whereas dystonia keeps on torturing me.*

I have long since realized that a hidden blessing of living with a prior health condition is the perspective that new life challenges, even life-threatening cancer diagnoses, are simply relative.

Feeling myself gradually cheering up, I even began to see some silver linings to exchanging my breasts. In addition to deciding that I would request my new ones to be a size larger than the ones that tried to kill me, I envisioned that they would finally match in size. Despite all the uncertainty and with those consolations in mind, I rode home, down cherry blossom-lined bike lanes, breathing in the sweet scent of new life in the air.

Several weeks before the operation, in a whirlwind of medical consults, I coordinated my reconstruction options with my surgeons. My mostly stoic cancer surgeon stated that she would only be removing my breasts. The following week, my tall, dark and handsome plastic surgeon, who clearly loved his job, explained that he would be giving me new ones.

Delighted that I did not have enough meat on my bones to use my own fat, muscle and skin tissues from my back, tummy or bum to shape the mass of my new breasts, he assessed me as a suitable candidate for a then-new, one-step breast reconstruction procedure using a mesh called AlloDerm® Regenerative Tissue Matrix. This mesh would hold my silicone implants in place immediately after my mastectomies. However, he couldn't be certain that my AlloDerm patches would be available in time.

In case they weren't, he offered to place standard temporary tissue expanders beneath the flat and tight muscles of my chest wall during surgery. These tissue expanders would then slowly be inflated over a matter of weeks, stretching the chest wall muscles. A few months later they would be replaced with semi-permanent implants in a second surgery.

I wouldn't know until the day of the surgery exactly which type of reconstruction — one-step or tissue expanders — I would be having and in what degree of breastlessness I would be waking.

As the weeks passed and I waited for my surgery date to arrive, I made one of the best decisions of my life. Despite my impending cancer treatments, I went ahead with my planned month-long trip with a friend through Southeast Asia. After feasting on spicy curries in Bangkok, cycling around the majestic Angkor Wat in Cambodia and trekking through a Malaysian jungle to picnic at a tea plantation, we would end up wearing our saris at another friend's traditional Sri Lankan wedding in Singapore. Life moves at a slower pace in that part of the world. Being there prepared me for the one-step-at-a-time adventure on which my cancer journey was taking me, and gave me a fresh perspective. *Living with cancer might not be that bad.*

My fortunes were indeed turning. As I was being wheeled into surgery, my saintly surgeon, dressed to impress in his hospital pastels and a halo-like cap, appeared above me. He quickly delivered the good news, "We've found some AlloDerm."

I won't be waking up flat-chested, I silently rejoiced, and thanked the previous owner of this patch of skin.

The tissue matrix — which is an inert geogrid-like mesh of

the skin from a dead body into which my own skin cells and blood vessels grow — was surgically attached to my muscles, shaped into two cups, and would serve as a type of internal bra for my semi-permanent implants. Having an internal bra forever alleviated the need for an external one. I could still wear a bra as an ornamental garment, or to get that little extra lift into my new cleavage, but I would no longer suffer bouncy or droopy breasts without that external support. The trouble, though, with having a permanent internal bra was that it would feel like I was always wearing a bra. The tight sensation would make me always aware of my breasts. This would be just another small price to pay for having forever perky boobs.

This benefit of bralessness also implicated the nipples. It is quite common that the nipples get removed during mastectomies. In a plumbing analogy, the Cancer Agency likens the nipple to the faucet at the end of a piping system that has been contaminated with a toxic substance: if you remove the pipes but leave behind the old taps, the contaminated parts from the old system are likely to contaminate the new one. And so the old nipples went too, leaving me with a dilemma: whether to install new, purely ornamental taps or not, in yet another surgery. Grafting new nipples with no reproductive purpose or sexually arousing sensation, only to need to wear a bra again in order to hide the permanently erect fake nipples, would completely counteract the braless perk of my new breasts. When the time came to make that decision, it was a relatively easy one.

Two years after my mastectomies, I still hadn't decided whether or not to install fake-fake-nipples in the form of a 3-D tattoo on each breast. Seizing the opportunity, my plastic surgeon offered my nipple-less breasts a modelling role for his intern to tattoo on my fake-fake-nipples, at no cost to me. Me and my breasts declined. I examined my slow-healing mastectomy scars that ran in two reddish-brownish lines across the width of my breasts, and considered that any future maintenance on my implants would reopen these scars. Either of these would surely muck up the fake-fake-nipple tattoos. It all added up to too much of a hassle.

I decided to get a different tattoo instead, one more uniquely symbolic of me. I chose the *Violator* rose and personalized it to exemplify the thorny nature of my life's journey and cancer experience.

My rose tattoo took root between my two new breasts on the third anniversary of my mastectomies, in a personal celebration marking my survival of the diagnosis and its treatments. Typically, some ritualistic festivity is reserved for the fifth anniversary of the main medical intervention, as it matches the statistical timeframe set by the cancer treatment establishment. But I like to do things my way.

The idea of a rose tattoo had planted itself before my operation while I prepared for the bodily disfigurement that was about to take place in the name of saving the rest of me. Among my research material was *The First Look* by Amelia Davis: a book containing brief personal stories and artistic photographs of women after their mastectomies. In addition to all my new technical knowledge about cancer, treatment and surgical practicalities, this book lent me some serenity about what I might look like; a sense of comfort that comes from giving shape to the feared unknown.

The image of a middle-aged woman with a lanky body similar to mine enticed me in particular. She stood sagely erect, with a tattoo in the shape of a rose over the scar where her left breast had once been. All the photographs in the book revealed elegance in their black and white versions of reality, but her tattoo presented an intentional addition of beauty where a real-life scar may otherwise scare some people with its raw severity. I liked the idea of adding such a symbol of gutsiness to my identity.

The thorns I designed for my *Violator* rose — so aptly termed to symbolize the various violations my body and spirit had endured — would ironically soften this image that I'd held for my life. Rather than being reminiscent of only pain and hardship, I made the thorns spiky but curved, revealing their gentler and more forgiving side. My cancer experience, while stressful and scary at times, has likewise led to desirable changes in my life and in my self-perceptions. It helped me to realize that while each of my life's thorns had been painful and prickly, each also came with blessings in disguise.

I can choose to reveal my cleavage and my rose tattoo to strangers, or not. Similarly, I can choose to share my cancer challenges if I wish. I cannot choose like this with my dystonia, because it is so visible. The insights on the medical approach and on my own body that I gained in my journey through cancer treatments enlightened me. So much so that since then, I have been able to make incredible improvements in my dystonic speech — ones that had been deemed by the medical experts for over two decades to be "impossible." What I have lost in spontaneity of not having a predictable voice because of dystonia, I gained in thoughtfulness and empathy for the challenges of others. I can see beauty where others may see only pain. But occasionally, I, too, forget that life, even with thorny challenges, can be beautiful.

My tattoo covers none of my breast cancer-related scars, although that remains a very beautiful possibility. After all, I designed the stem on my rose tattoo to look unfinished as I hadn't finished weaving in my mind the story of my experience when my anniversary and inking date arrived. Whether they are used to mask the fretful reminders of death or to celebrate one's commitment to life, I see tattoos as wonderful rituals.

It turns out that perhaps I need a few more life-affirming rituals to keep me from forgetting that my new breasts can still kill me. Mastectomy surgeries do their best to remove as much breast tissue as possible, but some always remains, and with it, a risk of recurrence. After my mastectomies in 2009, I made many changes in my diet, lifestyle and stress-coping mechanisms. I took chemotherapy and several natural immune-boosting treatments, learned about genetics and epigenetics of illness and health, and reconnected with the life-force within me. Curiously, in 2014, my boobs once more prompted me to reclaim the thorns on my not-all-rosy life.

For six months, my charmingly vigilant plastic surgeon and I had been monitoring a new lump that I discovered in my left breast. At that point, a second ultrasound could no longer rule out cancerous growth. Since this lump was so close to my implant, my surgeon would need to remove it completely to test it. Not wanting to spoil Christmas, we scheduled the surgery for Valentine's Day instead.

Still hopeful that my lump was harmless, I was nevertheless once more re-motivated to live fully and in the moment. I felt reminded that life could be over just like that. I again turned to travel while awaiting my surgery. Sensing that the stories of my life longed to be told, I met with a friend over New Year's for a writing retreat in the south of France to feed my cultural and culinary soul. I then joined a group writing retreat in Mexico to warm up that soul.

Two weeks after Valentine's Day, my surgeon's office emailed me the results just as I was heading out to meet with him. At this point, I was dying to find out. The wait always seems the worst. While exiting the lobby of my workplace, I scanned through the hefty jargon on my phone's tiny screen. *Extensive... Carcinoma... Infiltrating...* A tear spilled over my lower lashes as I looked up at my colleague greeting me on his way in from lunch. *Here we go again,* I thought as I cycled off past the early bloom of rosebuds for my hot date with my surgeon.

A few days later, my life changed again. I sat with my boss at the visitors' table in his bright penthouse office and used humour and an upbeat tone to ease the tension of telling him about my recent diagnosis. I was concerned about how my treatments would affect my work and relationships with my colleagues. No one at work knew about my diagnosis from five years before. I started that job after my previous cancer treatments had mostly finished. And even though it was challenging at times to continue my recovery in secret, I hadn't told anyone. I relished the feeling that at last I had a health issue that was invisible, unless I chose to share it, and that this, finally, made me like everybody else. I could not have this with my very visible dystonia.

For as long as I can remember, I have been labelled as abnormal and made to feel like there was something wrong with me. Only then, as I looked out the large window at the vast blue sky and explained to my boss how I dreaded telling my colleagues about my diagnosis because it was my cancer condition that finally made me feel normal, it dawned on me that I didn't need a life-threatening condition to normalize me. As I heard the words leaving my mouth, it occurred to me in that very moment that the story I'd been telling myself about the visible and invisible aspects of myself can be told differently. *I can choose what makes me feel normal, even if I can't always choose what others see!*

Confronting a breast cancer recurrence diagnosis less than five years after my first diagnosis is once again challenging me. I grapple with what it means for my lifestyle and for my longevity. I reassess what to do for a living and how much stress, compassion and joy to allow into each moment. Remarkably, with these additional transitions, my recurrence helps me re-confirm my commitment to life. I feel curious and excited that still more remains for me to discover and experience. And, I remind myself that, as if symbolically, one of the three dots tattooed on my chest, which were needed for the radiation treatment of my recurrence, aligns with the bottom of the unfinished stem of my *Violator* rose tattoo — hopefully placing the proverbial period on my cancer story.

MILKING MONTREAL –
HOW I SURVIVED THE CITY THROUGH BREASTFEEDING

Janine Alyson Young

Never does it occur to me that my breasts might somehow, one day, help me acclimatize to a gritty, alienating city like Montreal. From a young age they've always caused more trouble than they're worth. Too big, too heavy, too obvious. They stretch fabric, draw unwanted attention, and aggravate my back. While I rarely waste energy on body-image concerns, my breasts are the one complicated body part.

When at twenty-three my boyfriend Alex and I pack two thrift store trunks and leave Victoria, my breasts are the last thing on my mind. My soul is where the trouble lies. As we barrel away from the West Coast in a Greyhound bus, I realize I've made a terrible mistake moving to Montreal. I worry I'm falling farther and farther off-track and that I might never get right. In the first month, I go to shows, art openings, book launches, cafés, restaurants, buy wood-smoked bagels for the three a.m. walk home, and sign up for French lessons in the Plateau. We find an apartment in Saint Henri next to the tracks, explore the abandoned factories along the Lachine Canal, and watch the leaves blaze red as the autumn seeps in. But I still can't adjust. I find the city terribly lonely.

It's not until the cusp of my first Quebec winter when I become pregnant that Montreal starts to change. At first, it's harder. I am overwhelmingly sick and barely leave my apartment. The streets become a mental map of accessible washrooms and discreet alleys in case I need to vomit. The Market, the shops, every street corner assault my senses and stir my stomach.

But as my belly swells, the city begins to open up. Even strangers want to talk to me. English or French, it's doesn't matter: people want to tell me their stories. On the Metro a grandma confesses how much she misses her grandkids in France; a woman tells me about her traumatic birth and how her mother almost died; a man says he can tell I'm carrying a boy then wraps his arm around his teenage son and tears up.

Breastfeeding will eventually change my relationship with Montreal, too, but in the beginning of pregnancy I am dismayed to watch my breasts begin to swell. Like bread dough rising they grow and grow and it seems like they'll never stop. They — not so much my ballooning belly — become the epitome of pregnancy. They cause the greatest weight, become the most demanding to accommodate. Something about them makes me feel unwomanly. I feel, well, like a mammal. Worse, my breasts are not immune to sexual attention. On the street, in the Metro, men still burn holes with their eyes, lean in to announce their appreciation, and now this makes me especially squeamish. Shouldn't my body get respect for at least these nine months? Go call your mother!

❧❧

On a muggy August night, Sebastian Henri is born in Hopital de Lasalle. Barely a minute old, he's towelled off and placed on my chest. I don't look at him at first, my head back as I catch my breath. The doctors are working hard to control hemorrhaging, stitching second-degree tears. Shit, it stings. I'm raw and undrugged, and this prodding and needling is worse than the labour itself. I almost forget about my son, but then he is moving. His face is trying to reach mine and I lean down to greet him. He smells strange and unearthly, and I'm startled by how awake he is. He pushes his back up like he wants to crawl, then rubs his nose and lips over my skin and snorts like a strange creature. The nurses laugh. *C'est cute,* they say. I look at them and they point to my breasts, leaking thick and yellow colostrum for days already. I look down at this tiny being. Two minutes old and he knows what he wants. He wants milk.

❧

Back in our Saint Henri apartment, my milk comes in a couple of days later. I sink into the bath, breasts like rock sacks. Even after my body evens out the supply, I have abundant milk. Maybe too abundant. My already impossibly large breasts soften, fill, leak. Milk literally sprays from my breasts. If at any time I've wished for more subtle breasts, this would be it. But there's no hiding these babies. They're required and they're messy. They need to be whipped out what seems like a thousand times a day, and if I delay a feeding or two then milk simply spills forth and dampens my clothes.

Raising a baby in Montreal makes me anxious. I worry about things only a new parent can worry about: slipping on ice with him, being caught in the train for hours in a Metro shutdown (with, or worse, without him), getting mugged, the second-hand smoke from the downstairs neighbours, heatstroke, frostbite, bedbugs, tumbling down our steep narrow stairs, contaminated water from the old pipes and on and on. But there is one constant solace: wherever we go, whatever happens, I will be able to nurse my son.

❧

I get my first taste of on-the-run public breastfeeding during a two-hour wait at a medical clinic when Sebastian is seventeen days old. He's got a painful diaper rash and a goopy yellow eye, and I spend most of the wait for a drop-in doctor in the foyer, avoiding the packed waiting room. Sebastian is bundled in a carrier on my front and it's not long before I'm hot and sore and eager to drain the weight of milk pooling in my ducts.

I don't know where else to go, so I find a quiet washroom on the second floor. I close the stall door. There's no cover over the toilet bowl, so I tuck my dress between my legs and resist the forever-engrained urge to pee upon sitting on a toilet. Nursing is a relief as I lighten and he becomes full. But halfway through another woman settles into the stall beside me, and I become self-conscious. Not just of the intimate sounds of my son sucking and this private act suddenly becoming more public, but I'm also aware of what other feminists might say about me hiding away on a toilet. There's no way to please anyone with this breastfeeding thing, I think. Then I look down and see my son's eyes locked on mine as he drinks. Okay, I realize, so there's one person I can absolutely please with breastfeeding.

When the doctor finally sees us she refuses to look at him. He's too young, she says. I should have taken him to the ER at the Children's Hospital. On the long, hot, urban walk to the hospital Sebastian sleeps. He's content, and for that I'm grateful. But I'm exhausted. I haven't eaten or drank anything for hours, and the weight of carrying both a baby and my breasts on my front becomes excruciating.

When I arrive at Emergency, Sebastian's newness gives us status and we're whisked in, all the legitimately sick and injured children and their parents eyeing us. The diaper rash, it turns out, is a symptom of thrush, which is a yeast infection babies can get during birth, and is transferred to nipples during breastfeeding. The doctor asks if it hurts when I nurse. Yes, I admit. Sometimes my nipples crack and bleed. In the haze of life as a new mother I hadn't thought much about it. Through pregnancy and birth I've endured myriad discomforts. At the end of it all, we're given a prescription and some drops for the eye goop. The doctor asks if I've put any breast milk in his eyes. I'm confused. Breast milk, I learn, has an artillery of white blood cells, a super formula for healing.

Autumn arrives again and I marvel at the changes of the last twelve months. Sebastian and I have slow, quiet days wandering through Saint Henri. The vines that crawl up brick walk-ups ignite orange and red. The leaves in the park fall but the days are still warm enough. Alex and I adjust to life as three, and we begin to find our people. Some have children, some don't. The ones with kids embody a shared philosophy: babies don't stop you from having creative, ambitious lives. Babies simply join the fold, co-exist and add their own chaos. You take them with you wherever you go and they learn the ebbs and flows of life.

I get to know my neighbour Julia, a punk with a love for babies and tattoos, and her seven-month-old, Olive. We meet up every day, strap our babies to our bodies, and trek through the city. Something about being with Julia makes me feel like we're warriors. We hike all through the city. We change diapers and breastfeed publicly, daring someone to question us. The sight of Julia's tattooed breast becomes commonplace as she wanders the aisles of Village des Valeaurs or the grocery store. When Olive wants milk, she gets milk. Julia is the strongest, most badass woman I've ever met. When Alex and I leave Sebastian for the first time, it's Julia who looks after him. When he wakes up halfway through the evening, she even nurses him back to sleep.

One evening, my downstairs neighbour comes to the door. He looks awkward and embarrassed. I can't speak French well, and he stumbles over English but I realize he's asking for help. His girlfriend just had a C-section and can't breastfeed. She's trying but it's been days and she still has no sign of milk. I find her sitting at their kitchen table looking miserable, a tiny baby in a car seat on the floor. In terrible French, I try to encourage her. I get the impression that maybe he wants her to nurse more than she wants to, so I try to be gentle. I explain that because she's had a Caesarean her body's birthing hormones likely haven't kicked in and that it might take a week or more before she sees anything like milk. But, I hover over her and explain, unless she's stimulating her breasts to feed, her body might simply override the need for milk. It's supply and demand. The more you use, the more your body will make. She stares up at me and looks defeated. I leave them the pregnancy and baby books I've collected, and return later with a La Leche League pamphlet. What a failure of the medical system, I think. A can of formula magically appears in the mail of every expecting mother, but what about lactation consultants?

I don't want to pry, or make her feel like she's failed if she decides to bottle feed instead, so I force myself to leave them alone. I don't know if her milk ever comes in or if she gets help, but I run into them a few weeks later and they look much better than that first day home. I peer in at their pink little baby and ask what they named her. They glance at each other and the man tells me her name is my name. Her name is Janine.

❧

Breastfeeding becomes a new way to navigate Montreal. I prefer to be out in the city instead of a homebody, so sometimes I have to get creative with this whole baby thing. I discover I can nurse him while walking down the street without anyone noticing if I just keep him in the snuggly on my chest. This is often better than stopping on a bench or trying to negotiate my way into an establishment's washroom. I know that if I'm exhausted on a long walk home I am welcome to stop in at the knitting store on Saint Antoine and nurse on the couch. My boobs, for all the trouble they've caused over the years, often come in handy. On the odd night of horrible Montreal rush hour I can slip my screaming infant a boob and even the most prudish passenger in the car will breathe a sigh of relief. I gain a confidence I never had before, and I meet people along the way, women especially, who help me feel like I belong. Montreal is not the ideal place for the gentle, natural childbearing experience I crave, but over the months I find a way to navigate and negotiate the city that has left me battered and bruised so many times.

❧

One evening on the cusp of winter, Sebastian and I get stranded in Westmount because the Metro is down. I don't have a car seat to take a cab so I change him into his last dry diaper and start the hour walk home. Halfway home, he starts to wail. He's been in the stroller too long and he's hungry. I try to calm him without stopping. I just want to be home. I have knots in my back and I'm hungry, too. I think about walking all the way down through Saint Henri ignoring a screaming baby and know how crazy I'll feel. I sigh. We're in the No Man's Land area between Westmount and Saint Henri, the most unpleasant place I can think to stop. There's not even a sidewalk to pull off on, only the curb of the off-ramp. Sebastian's wails echo off the graffitied concrete overpass and the commuter train barrels along above us. In front of us rush hour streams off the 20. I want to cry, too. Sometimes Montreal is still too much.

Finally we just have to stop. I find a little patch of grass just beyond the overpass and take up my son. I sigh and whip a leaky boob out, suppress my own tears of exhaustion. He drinks and drinks. When he's quiet and content I take a deep breath and look around. Somehow, under the overpass and amongst the old shanties of Saint Henri, there is this little grassy knoll. I notice the sky is dusky and soft as the autumn moon appears above the brick rooftops. Down on the street, someone is even stringing gold lights in the Parisian Foundry. In that gritty, stunning way, Montreal can be beautiful and it always catches me off-guard. I stretch my legs out and relax. Somehow, in the grit of this city, we have everything we need to survive.

Your Boobs

Dina Del Bucchia & Daniel Zomparelli

must be covered up
must have retractable nipples
must be dealt with in post
must not be seen by teens
must wear a bra during all sex scenes
must be held up by a slightly out-of-date bra
must pretend to find comfort
must appear happy
should bounce around just enough to make them appear happy
should be alluded to
should be invisible
may be used as a comic element
may be used as a sex prop
may give a man a black eye for comedic effect
are abusive
are offensive
are the cause of MPAA ratings restrictions
are changing into fatty monsters
are twisting dicks into fleshy pretzels
are taking down whole cities
are crushing men
are destructive
are great orators capable of compelling other breasts to join
their cause with powerful speeches, commanding hand gestures,
and threats of genocide
will increase and decrease in size at will
will increase and decrease in aggression at will
will ruin the world
will cause the end of civilization

Strip, Reveal and Sex Appeal

Kelly S. Thompson

1. Officer Cadet Thompson's Impediment

I lie in the prone position, my C7 rifle balanced on sandbags, my chest pressed uncomfortably into the cold ground beneath me. The barrel points toward the target and I squeeze one eye shut, focus the sight on the intended destination of my bullets. I cock the semi-automatic and aim, finger hovering over the trigger. As I regulate my breathing the smell of CLP oil fills my nostrils. Last night I cleaned my weapon until traces of carbon laced my fingerprints.

"FROM 100 METRE RANGE, FIVE ROUNDS!"

My finger flicks off the safety switch in one smooth movement.

"PLATOON, AT YOUR TARGETS IN FRONT, AT YOUR OWN TIME, FIRE!"

A few more deep breaths before I fire my first five shots in a jolted sequence I hadn't prepared for. The rifle butt jerks erratically against my cheek. It will bruise. The result is a shit grouping with one bullet having missed the target entirely, the rest scattered like confetti across roundels of blue, white and red.

"What the fuck, Officer Cadet Thompson." The Master Bombardier flitters his greying moustache then moves down the line to scold some other ineffectual shooter.

"We're going to try that again," he shouts to us. "This time, try to hit the Goddamned targets."

"Hey, Thompson," says my platoon-mate. "Maybe it's just your tits getting in the way."

I feign my usual laughter and return focus to my weapon. Betty, I call her. Calm. Breathe in deep, breathe out slow. At that pause, that break between fresh air and faintness, I squeeze the trigger once. Twice. Five calculated times.

I get the second-highest mark in the platoon.

2. Captain Thompson's Source of Shame

I munch on a dry baby carrot, although as an officer at the Canadian Forces Military Intelligence School, I'm not supposed to be eating the graduation reception food. The ornate wood inside the officers' mess reveals the waterfront of Kingston through a wall of windows and a recently renovated patio, from which sun pours in and breeze does not. Apparently air conditioning is off the menu despite a mid-August heat wave and I'm sweating like mad in my scratchy wool uniform. My platoon commander eyes me and the carrot from her perch near the bar, sipping a ginger ale. Her disapproval thumps in the back of my head like a heartbeat.

"These things are so fucking boring, Ma'am," Shawn says. Master Corporal Robar. In public we have to pretend we aren't friends who call each other by first names.

I nod. "A parade for the sake of a parade."

Shawn pours himself a cup of coffee, slurps at it and makes a face. I could have warned him. "Why don't they just get out of here already so we can clean up and go home too?"

A line of newly minted Intelligence Officers, who will undoubtedly be deployed to Afghanistan within the year, mill around, chat, offer congratulatory slaps on the back.

"I'm going to walk around," Shawn says, jerking a thumb towards the creaky halls and adjusting his glasses. "Send in a search party if I fall asleep in the coat closet."

Shawn is the only person at the unit who is remotely close to my age. Our comrades sneer at us as though being in our early twenties is a mark against intelligence. In the military, wrinkles equal experience and inherent demanded respect. But at least Shawn has the required equipment between his legs. One less hurdle between ambivalence and acceptance.

My uniform tunic is too tight and the humidity is making it worse. It was last tailored to my thin post-basic-training body, back when I was eighteen, forcing me to bend awkwardly toward the veggie tray so I don't bust a seam. The gold buttons bulging near my chest threatening to burst across the room and hit my boss in the eye. The thought gives me a smirk of pleasure.

"Looking good, Ma'am. Lookin' good."

"Pardon?" I whip around, irritated.

"We don't usually see each other in dress uniform," he says, smacking his lips together. "You make it look awfully good."

He was a sergeant. Maybe a warrant. Possibly a fellow officer. They are all nameless, faceless pundits on my makeup, hair, body, as though every part of me is government property and worthy of commentary. Some of the come-ons are water off a duck's back, slipping into the murky pond of borderline harassment. Other remarks leave me wanting a shower, shameful. At twenty-five, three years after arriving at my first unit, I'm jaded. My boobs might as well be a medal on a flat chest, presented for valour in the face of countless unwanted sexual advances.

3. Kelly Thompson's Consolation Prizes

Water swirls around me, laps at my legs from my personal wake. The water is hot, too hot, stings my pink skin and sends a wobbly rash creeping near my thigh. The scar burns over the soft, palpable flesh to the left of my right kneecap. Near it, two other tiny scars, each a centimetre wide, the place where the orthopedic surgeon's arthroscopic tools explored the cavity of my leg, cut and sliced, vacuumed out debris while I lay awake and shivering on the operating table. Afterwards, I prayed my broken tibia would heal and I could purge the years of codeine and narcotics. But it's been ten years, and I'm in the tub unable to touch the scars that singe like a thousand elastics snapped against skin, exacerbated by an undercurrent of arthritic ache usually reserved for the elderly.

I feel whiny simply for hurting because soldiers do not complain about their injuries, even when those injuries result in a medical release; a loss of my military life. Our platoon T-shirts said, "Pain is temporary, Pride is forever." I'd long since balled mine up and stuffed it in the back of the closet.

The bath is my haven and nightly routine. I add scented oils, bubbles made of organic this and fancy-pants that, and then I slink my body into the dreamy concoction hoping that the heat, liquid and weightlessness will offer fifteen minutes of relief.

Underwater I feel jelly-like arms, thickening hips, soft round breasts, and pockets of fat on my back. All of it, this extra Kelly becoming increasingly visible over the last few years, is evidence of my injury, my inactivity, my emotional stumble since. I hardly recognize this version of myself, although her nakedness is stark and glittering in expensive bath products. My consolation prizes are near-perfect breasts. They're swollen from weight gain, fleshy orbs that bob atop the water with small nipples shrivelling as they break water like a whale blowhole before retreating under the popping bubbles.

But they, too, are flawed. One nipple easily grows hard with cold and stimulation, as it should, but the other sucks in like Grandpa's lips without his dentures. Despite my double-D breasts, I've always worn padded bras so that a high-functioning air conditioner doesn't accidentally reveal my secret. And the short list of partners to whom I revealed my nudity was given a warning in advance. *Hey, I have this thing,* I'd say, clutching my bra to my chest before the big reveal. *An innie.* A what? *An innie.* Like your belly button? *Uh, yeah, kind of.* In the past, men had tried to tease my nipple into a state of attention, convinced dedication would equate sexual prowess. An unspoken challenge. But Innie is stubborn like the body it's attached to. I read an article once that said men are subconsciously attracted to women who have symmetrical bodies. Another strike against me in the criteria of attractiveness.

"How're you feeling, hun?"

Joe hands me a cup of tea and kisses the top of my head. My hands automatically cover my waist, the rolls of fifteen extra pounds. His bald head attracts the moisture from the steam and he swipes at his face. I shrug my shoulders and swish my legs back and forth, reach to tug the shower curtain closer. Our bull terrier, Pot Roast, comes in to join the family party, stares with beady black eyes that seem to look past the pounds and through to the insecurity that bubbles underneath.

"Let me know if you need anything," he says. His wedding ring catches the exposed-bulb lights and I reach out until our fingertips connect as Joe moves into the bedroom across the hall to prepare his uniform. Convinced my extended arm is an invitation, Pot Roast is quick to fill the empty space and stretches his stumpy neck over the barrier of the bathtub, leaving a smear of stray black and white hairs on my palm.

"I've decided, officially. I want to sign up," I call out to Joe. He attaches his Velcro nametag to his uniform — the uniform I used to wear too — then comes to lean against the bathroom doorjamb.

I'd spent the majority of the evening looking at the Vancouver Burlesque Centre website, fantasizing about classes to sculpt a body from this lump of clay. Nerves settle in the back of my throat, acidic and thick now that the commitment has been made out loud because society dictates my clothes belong on my body, not left in a Hanzel and Gretel-esque trail of seduction. I stress about jaywalking. My bills are always paid on time. And I am a military officer still. And yet I am not.

"You should," Joe says, smiling with encouragement. "It'll be fun."

❧

I arrive at the Vancouver Burlesque Centre feeling sick to my stomach and winded from the ten steps to the front door, which fills me with ominous dread. In the studio off East 6th Street, women chat amongst themselves, as wide ranging in age as they are in shape. Some thicker, some thinner. Some tall, some short. I fall somewhere in between; short blond hair, five foot seven, curvy and soft.

Laughter fills the room as ladies stretch and warm up, bending for their toes, leaning into calf stretches. I consider leaving right then before anyone even notices me, because what would be the shame in it? Who cares that I paid one hundred dollars for the classes?

"Welcome to class, everyone. I'm Lola Frost, your instructor, and welcome to Advanced Chair Progressive. Shall we do a little warm-up?"

Lola swallows a room whole, her black hair shiny like an olive and stark against pale skin. Muscles stretch firm over a masculine frame that is also feminine in the way she moves, giggles like someone fifteen years younger, clacks her artificial nails that are adorned with sparkles and sharpened to a dull point. She even holds her hands as though mid-performance, tapping at her iPod using the pad of her pointer finger *just so.*

I saw Lola perform at the Rio, an old theatre that sometimes hosts live performances. I paid thirty dollars for my ticket, clutched it to my chest then watched as she twirled and spun, leaving a trail of shed clothing behind her. Lola exudes sex, but also something else, feminism perhaps; an invitation to call her out for getting naked and calling it anything but art. I want to reach out and touch her hand, somehow transfer some of that elegance in a swift motion of osmosis.

We go around the room and I learn the names of my new comrades. There is Lil' Bo Peek, Ruby Danger, Venus Desire. There are no Jessicas or Beths or Donnas.

"So, before we get going, we're all working toward performing at our Student Showcase, correct? Everyone wants to take the stage?"

We collectively nod, some more assertively than others. I am ready, I tell myself, fists clenched and teeth grinding to dust. Once, I'd made a career out of being brave, hadn't I? I want to feel stares burning holes in what is left of my clothing. I want spotlights and glitter and glam. I want someone other than my husband to regard me as sexy. *I* want to regard me as sexy.

"Well, let's get going then with a warm-up. Now, Kelly, you mentioned you have a knee injury, right? I'll show you different adaptations to help with pain. Okay?"

A pulse of 1920s music fills the room. We start the warm-up and I quickly feel out of my league, although I refuse to let anyone know I'm sweating it, other than the obvious fact that I'm literally drenching my Lululemon tank. We do an eternity of pliés and squats, which I mostly do using only my left leg, and then crunches. So. Many. Crunches. There are delicate arms lifts, yoga moves, neck rolls and stretches. I want to die. I will not make it. Go on without me, troops. Leave me behind like the dead weight that I know I am!

"So, everyone feeling that? You feeling that burn?"

I cannot catch my breath to offer an answer. I chug back half my Nalgene bottle of water and wipe damp palms down the front of my leggings, leaving a smear of glitter left over from the previous class, an unoffending dusting of pixie sass.

The music changes to a new beat, something deep and throaty that rumbles with bass. Lola throws her right leg up onto the chair, her toes landing softly on point, and tosses her head while delicately clutching the back of the chair, cocks her hip and winks at the non-existent audience.

"So first things first. When doing hairography, you want to hold on to the chair so you don't knock yourself over with your own awesomeness," Lola says, and I am aware that she is only partially joking.

"I'm not sure about my own awesomeness," I say, a burp of nervous laughter escaping.

"No, no, we don't do that," one of my classmates says, wagging a finger. "We are all awesome here."

Kindly silenced, I nod in response and unfurl my arms that are wrapped protectively around my waist. We spend the next hour crafting our routine, chatting about costumes and practising move after painstaking move. Afterwards, Lola thanks us for coming and I pack up my yoga mat and kneepads, slog them over my shoulder and trudge toward freedom.

"So," Lola says, halting me in my tracks. I am so close to the door. I am close to food and water and Epsom salts and Tylenol. "How was your first class? Enjoy it?"

"I did. It was so much fun."

I feel bad for lying because she is Lola Frost and I sense one does not mess with this kind of badassness. And yet as the words leave my lips, I realize they are true. For the first time in ten years, I am exhausted, sore, hungry and injured and yet simultaneously happier than I've ever been.

4. G.I. Jiggles Takes 'Em as They Are

"How was it?" Joe asks, voice full of hope.

I answer by showing him some of my new moves on a dining room chair, the best I can though I'm limping badly. I "Dip My Chip," a slow curve of my spine and pop of my fleshy bum, and "Sexy Jellyfish," which involves balancing on my tailbone and flailing my arms and legs in slow, fluid movements. And the greatest lesson of all. Always. Shake. Boobs. I am deterred only momentarily when my shirt rides up and my back skids against the wood frame. Then I peel down my pants, because that's what I've been taught to do today, to proudly reveal my new war wounds, fleshy purple bruises the colour of eggplants. He kisses my battle-scarred hips then runs me a hot bath, extra bubbles.

Swishing in the bathwater, I create a list of to-dos as the show date draws near.

1. Find costume
2. Ensure costume shows the good parts and hides the bad parts
3. Accept that there are no bad parts
4. Paint toes and nails
5. Wax everything possible
6. Buy Tylenol, Advil and numbing cream for item number 5
7. Devise a Burlesque Name

My sister supports my naked venture over the phone while breastfeeding her new baby across the country in Ontario. She suggests Arthritica Vulcan.

"You get it? Like arthritis?"

"I get it."

"You don't like it?"

"I'm trying to be sexy, Meghan," I say with a sigh.

"Point taken. Isn't your stripper name supposed to be like, the name of your first pet with the street you lived on as a kid?"

"Kaiser Scott?" I say, testing the name out loud. "I don't

think I want to be associated with the German regime either."

We toss names back and forth from ideas promulgated by various online generators. And then it comes to me. Military. Tough. Jiggly curves. Demi Moore for God's sake. G.I. Jane.

"How about G.I. Jiggles?"

"Perfect," my sister says. "Just don't let anyone call you G.I. Don't want you getting mixed up with a gastrointestinal infection."

"Jiggles it is."

5. They've All Come Full Circle

Guilt & Co is the perfect bar location for underbelly art. Tucked under a humming restaurant in Vancouver's Gastown, it seeps history with exposed brick and an intimate setting. Most of the patrons are tucked close to the bar, ordering drinks before the show begins. My skin itches and tingles like a crack addict, a tick I soothe with champagne and Blue Buck pints.

"You're going to do great," Joe says.

My garter belt itches underneath my pinup-style dress, a light lavender colour with a black ruffle around the chest. The saleslady told me it complimented my shape and said she'd kill for my curves, to which I said "thanks," without my typical self-deprecating clip. My short hair is stiff with hairspray and juts out in a million directions and I've clipped in a purple feather flower that I wore on my wedding day.

"I should go get ready."

Joe gives my bum a pinch and I slip backstage to a flurry of breasts, lipstick and sequins, making me feel like I've stepped into a Las Vegas chorus line practice. There is no shame in a burlesque dressing room as rolls of carpet tape and tubes of latex glue are passed around for adhering pasties. The pasties, like the nipples they adorn, vary greatly. One lady wears clamshell shapes that remind me of Ariel in *The Little Mermaid*. Mine are purple, sequined and tasselled, the brownish-pink edge of my areola slightly visible upon closer inspection. I attach the tape and work Outie nipple until it protrudes, then press on the disc of fabric. But damn Innie refuses to budge into pert action. Logistics Officers are prepared for everything and yet I had not anticipated this.

"Just slap some more tape in there, honey," says a larger woman wearing a fluffy boa. Her bare breasts slap together like a pair of gorgeous Liberty Bells. "Here." She snips the tape expertly, filling in the area where my pointed nipple should be. She layers multiple strips until she's built up the sticky layer to her satisfaction. "Now try that."

She does not turn away as I press my breast into the quarter-sized dab of covering. Her handiwork is perfect.

"Give 'em a tug. Make sure they'll stay."

I pull at the tassels but my nipples remain unseen. The target of my sexuality covered just enough to keep the audience guessing.

"That's great, thanks," I say, somehow embarrassed, somehow not.

"We've all got our thing, right?" She pats her oversize bottom, which is decked out in some kind of beaded skirt. A swish of her rear reveals a sequined G-string underneath. "Break a leg."

If only she was aware of the irony.

Women push to get close to the mirror for last-minute touch-ups and I nudge my way to the rest of my group, seven other brave, beautiful women. We crowd around each other to do up straps, tuck in tags, hook stockings to garters. Ready for the attack. On stage, Lola is proudly introducing us to the audience and I take a final look in the mirror. Fishnet stockings ebb from underneath my waist-high booty shorts and my jewelled fake eyelashes shimmer an SOS in the reflected light. My velvet vest buttons are precariously done up around my chest, which is hardly contained by the lacy bra underneath. I heft each breast in my hand to adjust for maximum cleavage, smiling when my bedecked fingernails skim the edge of the pasties. Removal of the fabric discs will be no walk in the park. I've heard horror stories of blisters and necessary hours of tub soaking to ease extraction. Like adorning pasties in the first place, each dancer has their preferred method to get them off. It will hurt, I'm told, but no matter. *Pain is temporary.*

Ready. Aim. Fire.

THE FRIEND WITH BOOBS

Ruth Daniell

In grade eight I had a chenille sweater striped with burgundy, pink, tan and white that I loved to wear with dark jeans. I felt particularly stylish in this outfit because I had a pair of striped socks that just happened to have the same colour scheme. I once wore them and the sweater together, and one of the popular girls noticed and told me it was cool that they matched. It seems ridiculous now, but that kind of comment could keep me fuelled for months. I was eager to be admired. I didn't care about being popular but I was eager to make friends. Grade eight was a new school, full of girls (and boys) from different neighbourhoods who hadn't known me in elementary school and didn't know I was a loser. Cooties may not be real, but they have very real effects if the in-crowd diagnoses you with them in the third grade. It can take years to make a full recovery. I had a great home life, but I still didn't have any friends at school.

I had read in a beauty magazine that flat-chested women should wear horizontal stripes because it can help disguise the lack of breasts. I took this advice to heart.

My hometown in northern BC has long winters. It must have been March or April. The air was still cool, but it was starting to smell like spring, even though there were patches of snow on the ground. It was warm enough that I didn't have to wear a coat at lunch hour; I could walk out the wide double doors at the rear entrance of the school wearing my burgundy-striped fuzzy sweater and be perfectly comfortable. I remember feeling the early spring wind blow through the fabric to my skin, and as I opened the door I imagined that my hair blew behind me as if I were in a shampoo commercial.

"Nothing," I heard someone say.

"Medium, big, nothing," the boys listed. I understood. A small

198

group of guys had perched just outside of the doors to rate the breast size of each girl that came out.

I was wearing my favourite sweater. But I was nothing.

In grade ten I still didn't have boobs, but I finally had the kind of BFF friendship I had always wanted with a girl who was decidedly much cooler than me. I'd always wanted to be inseparable with someone. I wanted a friend who would do cliché best-friend things with me like the fashionable teenagers in TV commercials: have sleepovers, talk about boys, paint our fingernails, bake cookies and watch movies and shop for clothes. Jill had just moved from Manitoba, and she had a lilt to her voice. I couldn't decide if it was some kind of accent or not. She wore makeup. She had long, beautiful brown hair and puppy eyes, and big, soft-looking triangular breasts. Her breasts were the first things I noticed about her; the first day she sat next to me in career and personal planning class she was wearing a pale-blue, skinny-striped shirt that had laces up the front that criss-crossed to just below her collarbones, but nevertheless provided peeks at her skin from her torso up. Ever since my failure with my fuzzy sweater from grade eight, I had pretty much given up on dressing cool. I wore outfits that hid my body, and certainly nothing like what Jill wore. She was daring without being tacky. She was cool, but she was new to town and hadn't yet been scooped up by any other social groups. I knew that her getting assigned next to me in career and personal planning class was meant to be.

Jill is the type of person who needs to be needed; I think I was as much a project to her as anything else. I didn't mind being her makeover project, though, because I finally had default social plans every day after school and every weekend. I let her style me. I started wearing tank tops and the hip-hugging jeans that all the other girls were wearing (instead of the painter's pants I had been favouring for two years). I even started wearing skirts. I didn't have any breasts, but I was proud of my legs. Some of the boys who remembered me from elementary school still shoulder-checked me in the hallways to whisper "dyke," "loser" and "wannabe," but I was bolstered by the fact that Jill, at least, thought I was worth her time. Besides, the rest of the school knew I was her best friend. Jill's best friend. It was the best social standing I had ever had.

⚓

Near the end of high school, one of the other girls from our tentative friend group who had more permissive parents started having parties in her backyard most weekends. In theory, the parties were interesting because her parents had vodka coolers we were allowed to drink, but most of us were still too straight-edge to consider it. Instead, the highlight was the full-sized trampoline we'd all sink into — boys and girls — our limbs criss-crossing thrillingly, butterflies fluttering in our guts. So many opportunities for accidental touching and hand-holding in the dark. The stars were right above us, like silver-coloured fish, mirror images of us gathered into our own net. Sometimes there was so much static electricity that the sparks between us when we touched actually snapped silver for milliseconds at a time like hooks.

One evening we decided to do imitations. I don't remember who started it. Nobody wanted to be mean, so the caricatures performed weren't especially hilarious. Someone pretended to be me by babbling about English class in one long, over-excited run-on sentence. I was known for getting good marks and being too eager about school. The impression got some laughs.

I thought I might be able to be funny too. I stood up in the centre of the trampoline. I imagined that I felt drunk, although I had not had a single sip of anything except water. The trampoline was sagging under our collective weight, and I had to concentrate to keep my feet from sliding together. Everyone else sat cross-legged around the edge of the trampoline. Our host's parents had a string of Christmas lights hanging off the back of the porch behind us. I remember noticing that the lights curved off the staircase railing reminiscent to the way a bra strap slips off a girl's shoulder, and that someone I didn't know was smoking a cigarette.

I shifted my feet again, and then I turned around until I saw Jill on one side of the trampoline. I stared pointedly at her breasts for several full seconds.

"You're Billy!" someone guessed.

"Yes!" I said.

The group howled; Billy was a boy at school who consistently failed to be subtle about where his eyes landed.

"What?" Jill shrieked, pretending to be horrified but obviously pleased.

"He's always staring at you!"

"Yeah, he's always looking at your rack."

"Nailed it!"

"Hilarious!"

"What a perv!"

"Ew," Jill said. "I can't believe I hadn't noticed."

She had noticed. Jill was the friend with boobs. I was the friend with straight As. It did not occur to either one of us to be offended with either of these labels.

The brand-new, stylish me — the boobless me who had still been a knockout during the grade twelve grad fashion show, sharing the catwalk with Jill — was a me that existed because of Jill. We were like a couple. Most sentences about either one of us were finished with the other person's name. Ruth and Jill, Jill and Ruth. But Jill was like a sister; her parents worked shift work so she often came home after school and had dinner with my family, and my dad taught her to downhill ski so she could come with us on our family spring break trips to Banff or Jasper and hit up the mountains. By the time high school was over, my identity as a woman had formed in comparison to Jill. She was the friend with boobs. The friend who could voice her opinions, loudly, at whoever would listen. The brave one. And I was the flat-chested, quiet girl who only got chatty about books. I was loved for it, for being that girl. I found a sureness, a confidence, in that role. And I was happy.

❧

Jill stayed in Prince George when we graduated, but I moved away to Victoria for university to study writing. We remained close the first couple years through phone calls and instant messenger and my trips home during the summers, but — buoyed by my best-friend status with Jill — I now had the social confidence to make new friends at university without her. Her makeover project was a success. I didn't need her anymore. I still wanted her, but want isn't the same as need, and she began to lose interest in me. She became even more interested in boys, in getting and maintaining their attention. She liked making them stare, she liked teasing them, she liked dancing with them, she liked their eyes on her breasts. Her identity had formed around her ability to capture males' attention. I don't know if she ever felt sorry about that, but a couple of years after I moved away, she went missing; she had gone away with a man much older than her who made promises he couldn't keep.

I worried about her constantly but I also continued as I had been, wearing my newer, better sweaters with horizontal stripes, writing poems, and eventually falling in love. My husband says he remembers one of our first conversations in second-year university after an English honours seminar one afternoon; he recalls noticing that I had full, big round breasts, but I insist he must be conflating memories. I was barely nineteen then. Less than four months before, I had visited another friend in Vienna; in most of the photos from the trip I am wearing a pink skirt that Jill had helped me pick out and a white tank top with no bra — and no need for one.

By the end of our degrees, James and I were sharing a tiny apartment in Cook Street Village and sharing a single closet. Over the years I had been frugal, and not acquired much in the way of new clothes. For the most part, I was still wearing the wardrobe that I had accumulated under Jill's guidance in high school, with only the occasional new cardigan or simple dress. One of the only changes that I had made, out of necessity, was changing bra sizes. I had grown out of A-cups fairly soon, and hadn't thought much of it when I moved into a B-cup. B wasn't big. I was still small-chested. When my B-cups started getting uncomfortable, though, I had to eventually make the move into a C-cup. I remember reasoning that C was "average": not small, I guessed, but not big either. I hadn't heard from Jill in months. I tried not to, but I worried about her every day.

❧❧

When my parents came to Victoria to attend our May convocation ceremony, they also took me clothes shopping as a kind of graduation present. I didn't feel good in any of my clothes, especially my blouses, and my breasts nearly always felt tender and I did not understand why. After an offhand remark about how uncomfortable jogging was, my mother insisted that our first stop was to a department store to find me a new bra or two.

I remember standing in the Sears changing room with a bright-eyed woman with short dark hair who cheerfully asked me to take off my shirt.

She eyed my bra. "So what size do you wear?" she asked.

"I'm a C-cup," I said.

The sales clerk's eyes swept over my chest again. "Oh, honey," she said, "Those are not Cs."

Yes, they are, I thought furiously. Anything else was definitely big. And I did not have big boobs. I was the friend with little boobs. I was the bookish, quiet friend who had no boobs. And somewhere — though I didn't know where — Jill was out there. The friend who had boobs and men's attention. The clerk must have seen how stunned I looked, because then she said, "I hate to break it to you but we're looking at double Ds for sure."

She brought me several different bras. One of them had subtle lace on the band and practical, soft full cups with a simple pearl bead decoration between them that did not seem too quaint. To my surprise, I liked how I looked in it. I felt supported. Different. But good different. I found I was standing straighter; I wasn't slouching my sore shoulders. I felt taller. I bought it in both colours, ivory and black.

I wasn't a flat-chested girl anymore. I suppose I had known that my old definition, my glorious role as Jill's best friend, wasn't really accurate now, but I hadn't accepted it. I knew I wasn't a shy, quiet girl. But I hadn't been ready to admit that I was a woman with big boobs. I had gotten so comfortable with my identity as a small-busted woman that I didn't even realize how uncomfortable my body was as I insisted on wearing too-small bras.

"You have a lovely shape," the clerk said. "And doesn't that feel better?"

It did. And it continued to feel good. With a properly supportive bra, I now found I wasn't as sore. It was a revelation: I had big breasts! Me! Who knew?

"Well, I've always appreciated them," James pointed out. I laughed.

❧

Less than three months after my life-changing bra-fitting experience, I got a phone call from Jill, who told me that she had left the older man and come home. I cried in relief — she was safe — and then, less than two months after that, I moved back home, too. After spending years on the Island near his family, James and I had decided to spend the year in Prince George before going to grad school. I was nervous about what it would be like to be in the same city as Jill after so much time. She had been the one with the boyfriends and the boobs and now I had a serious boyfriend and big boobs. Maybe we wouldn't even recognize each other.

We did, of course, although we could no longer fall into our familiar roles. We didn't fit them anymore, any more than I fit into a C-cup bra.

I worked on my writing that year, and got a part-time job at the local Sears in the lingerie department where I got certified as a professional bra fit consultant. A semi-retired woman named Norma mentored me. She was so knowledgeable that she had people from Smithers and Quesnel who drove into Prince George just to buy their bras from her. It didn't surprise me. I knew how much the no-nonsense, sensitive guidance of the clerk from Victoria had helped me to confront a realistic, and more loving, understanding of my own body.

The first woman I helped get into a comfortable bra was a cancer-survivor in her eighties who gently pointed out her scars and said she didn't like to have any seams rubbing on them. I got to run through the basics with a transgender woman who had never purchased a bra before. Once, a young woman with red hair and very fair skin burst into tears when I fitted her with a wireless A-cup; apparently, wired B-cups had been chafing her skin for months. "I had kind of assumed I'd always just be a little bit in pain," she confessed to me. I was full of gratitude; helping these other women made me feel a comradery that was much different from the intense intimacy I had once known with Jill. And helping other women with their bras reinforced the new tenderness with which I regarded my own full breasts. I eventually had all of the brand names and styles memorized, until I could — just as quickly as the sales clerk in Victoria — glance at a woman's chest and gauge what size she was and which models would be likely to best support her shape. About nine months after being in Prince George, Jill gave birth to her first child. I picked out her nursing bras for her. She didn't need me to, but it was a sweet gesture, so long after the years she had spent bossing me into outfits in similar changing rooms.

I'm not twenty-three anymore; I'm no longer lithe and skinny, and a double-D doesn't cut it. I usually only find adequate support in speciality bras that cost one hundred and fifty dollars and just come in beige. I begrudge my breasts' size when I have to climb up and down stairs, fit into a bathing suit, or attempt jogging.

Boobs

They get sore and tender and in my way. I half-dread the size they'll reach if I ever decide to get pregnant. I'll probably never wear anything much more daring than that pale-blue shirt with the criss-cross laces in the front that Jill once wore. I generally avoid accentuating my breasts in any way, but I don't hide them either. I have a couple of sweaters with horizontal stripes and I know I look fabulous.

Miriam in Mexico, Postpartum

Esther Griffin

The bassinet rustles.
His tiny feet kick
the mosquito netting
and my sister stiffens.

Small chirps grow
into the beginnings of a cry,
as his fists wind up overhead.
She stands, adjusts her tummy
girdle, smooths her shirt.

I recognize the trill
of hunger after a long
sleep. She mumbles she's overdue
for a shower and floats away
on the current of her baby's cries.

I stand rocking him.
He's been in my arms
for two hours. On this earth
for 27 days. His curled limbs

sweat through to my skin.
His beating heart, a song
of our shared blood.
And together, we dance.

Boobs

He loves to bob and sway. Mesmerized
by the patterns of tile and light
on the ceiling, he stretches his downy head
into the curve of my palm. I long
to inhale him into my body.

❦

I hand him over, and she fidgets
him into her arms. He cries
from the disruption. Only
from being moved.

He hates my boney, flat chest,
she says. *He wants the cushion
of your breasts.*

She holds him out to me, chubby legs
peddling. His face roots
back, neck wobbling
towards her milky smell.
The pulse of his mother.

He doesn't know bone from flesh,
I start to say, but she's already flown.
And as his warbles rise, I hold
him to the ache
of my empty breasts.

NINE

Lynn Easton

Salt sticks to our arms. The hot wind swirls around us like the waves lapping at our legs. Jesse's blond mess of hair is bleached white from weeks of sea and sun. I see this. She sees only the sea.

She searches for anemones that close and open around her finger with the grace and strength of something sensual she loves but doesn't yet understand. She is hot. Wants to swim. She is going in, but first she begins to remove her shirt. I reach toward her, and begin to speak. Then stop. We are not alone on the beach because she is with her friend Michael. They are nine. The magic number that hovers over girls like a school marm, leans over curling its wagging finger, warning of consequences. Nine — the age when breasts start to matter, when bathing suits will be worn, and towels will be used as changing-room tents.

The boy turns to his mother for an explanation. His mother shrugs her shoulders apologetically and they both look away. I am paralyzed on shore as Jesse throws me her shirt. We have only recently moved to this small West Coast island and I am unsure of the rules of etiquette.

But I know the rule of nine.

I watch Jesse in the ocean. I have been meaning to talk to her about her penchant for taking off her clothes — but I can't do it. I can't tell her she needs to cover up her non-existent breasts. It's not some grand altruistic gesture — I just can't.

❧

Michael and Jesse are distracted by their search for life below the surface. They don goggles and snorkels and breathe deep gasps of discovery. Oblivious in their skin. Slipping through the water like the seal that watches from the other side of the waves. Jesse is no mermaid. She is muscle and movement. The hair on her arms shines in the sun. She closes her eyes and kicks her feet hard to stay afloat. They both jump over the waves and the seal slips away.

Jesse calls for a shirt when she is done. Jumps from one foot to another to keep warm on the way home. She drops her clothes on the deck of our home like she's taking off her coat after a long day's work. She struts. Still nine. Still nude.

I learn the rule of nine on a sunny afternoon in 1971 as I strut around my backyard. I fiddle with a small branch from our backyard maple. It's going to be a bow. Or an arrow. I am not sure. I whittle the end with my pocket knife. Hum. It is hot and the air feels warm on my skin.

I climb the tree that looks across the alley into the neighbour's yard. I see Dwight. Thirteen. A blowhard and a braggart. I ignore him. But I can't ignore my mother who calls me from the back deck. This is unusual — she rarely calls me — so I go.

"You need to put a shirt on." She is not loud or angry. "You're nine. You need to wear a shirt even in the summer." Her voice is quiet. Her head is down.

"I know it doesn't make any sense, I know."

"Then don't make me."

She doesn't say anything.

"No, I won't do it."

She has never made me do anything in my life. She leaves me alone. That's what I like about her. But today is different; today she is resolute and uncompromising.

"You have to."

"No, I don't."

But in this moment, I know I do. In this moment, I am disgusted with my mother. Her weakness. Her lack — of protection, of loyalty, of chutzpah. I know this decree has something vaguely to do with my flat chest and the breasts that will grow there someday soon. But that doesn't feel like the whole story. I am embarrassed to be a girl and I don't understand why. I don't want to understand.

My mother sits with me on the deck as we look at the tree I was called out of.

I don't say a word. She thinks I am mad.

"When I was nine, I had to stop climbing trees," she says. "That was my very favourite thing. I felt like I was on top of the world. But my dad came to me one day and said, 'No more climbing trees. You are nine. That's it.'"

She looks at me close in the eye. I can't tell if she is sad, or mad or somewhere in between. "I will never tell you to stop climbing trees, but I *have* to tell you to put your shirt on. You need to get used to it."

⋘⋙

As I watch Jesse swim, I feel for my mother drowning as she forced me into those clothes. Even so, she wasn't about to pile on the same shame that was inflicted on her. I realize the look I saw in my mother's eyes that day was defiance. She could give me that much. She could let me climb.

I worry about how far I can kick the rule of nine down the road. Move the line forward. Whatever I do, it won't be far enough for Jesse. I will see the look I gave my mom. It will hurt like those willowy weapons I used to carve out of new growth: fast, quick and true. Still, I will try to defy — for both of them. I may be kidding myself, it may just be cowardice, but I can't say the words to Jesse. Here on her beach where she is most free. Most herself.

There's a group of old women on this island that still meets on the shore of Chickadee Lake to swim each week. Nude. The waves lap at their legs as the hot wind swirls. Their grey hair hangs down over where their breasts used to be, and their breasts hang below that.

They laugh loud and contagious, and I am reminded of my mother and my mother's laugh. I watch them from across the lake where I live with my daughter and remember my mother's eyes

211

when she told me she'd never stop me from climbing trees. The older women continue to laugh. Unapologetic. Defiant. Jesse and I listen to their voices echo off the hillside.

They dive like water nymphs off an old log, sleep in the sun when they are done. They swim like seasoned Olympians across the lake, tread water in the deep, and chat with equal ease.

Jesse and I sit on a makeshift bench made out of an old cedar. It feels like a sanctuary — our secret spot. I lie by the lake and listen. Close my eyes and still see the older women lying naked on dead tree trunks, their wrinkled breasts resting atop their bodies like fading beacons, recharging in the sun. Did these women always defy the rule of nine? Or did it take years of deliberate bravery to drown their shame at the centre of the lake?

Jesse scrambles up the bank to get as high as she can above the waves. Climbs the maple that has the rope swing. Holds tight and wraps her legs around the solid knot. She flies outward over the water in the direction of the old women.

She lets go.

Points her arms into the air above her flat, tanned, bare chest. I watch her enter the silk of the black lake like a golden arrow.

"How was that one, Mom? What's my score? What's my score?"

"Nine point nine nine," I shout.

Damned near perfect.

Origin Stories

Nancy Lee

AA

I am an explorative and hungry toddler. I routinely break out of my playpen in search of anything that resembles food. One day, my mother discovers me at her bedside table polishing off an entire packet of birth control pills. Another, she finds me wailing beside the open refrigerator, hands and mouth smeared red with extra hot Chinese chili sauce. A highly superstitious registered nurse, my mother worries the extreme heat of the chili sauce coupled with the birth control hormones will create a strange and unpredictable chemical reaction in my body. As in most matters, she is right.

A

As a child, I never dream of having a woman's body. I grow up in a house with three older boys. The dynamic between us is this: I will do anything to spend time with them; they will do anything to get rid of me. My eagerness makes me prone to mishaps. I fall into mud puddles, get splinters under my fingernails, swallow prized marbles.

I prefer pants to skirts and resent any outfit that causes my mother to warn, "Don't get that dirty." I have short hair and permanently scraped knees.

My one concession to girlhood, a baby doll called Teeny Tiny Tears, who I cuddle and scold in equal measure, nurses from a plastic bottle, not from my imagined breasts.

B

I am nine years old, staring at my reflection in the mirror of a Sears change room. The thin straps and flimsy polyester of a 32A brassiere cinch my chest. Flesh bulges along the lines of elastic.

My mother knocks on the other side of the door. "Does it fit?"

"No."

"Too big?"

"Too small."

"Let me see."

"No."

"Are you sure it doesn't fit?"

"Yes."

I hear my mother talking with the sales clerk. Her tone is apologetic. Another box slides under the change room door. I check the label, 36B, the same size my mother wears.

At school, they call me Dolly Parton. They will get more creative.

C

Breasts: Airbags. Assets. Balloons. Bazangas. Bazooms. Belly awning. Bomb shells. Boobies. Bosom. Boulders. Breastules. Bristols. Bust. Cachongas. Cans. Cantaloupes. Chest. Cleavage. Funbags. Gazangas. Grapefruits. Headlights. Hee-Haws. Honkers. Hooters. Hot Mamas. Juggs. Knockers. Lungs. Mammaries. Mamoos. Manchesters. Melons. Missiles. Mounds. Mountains. Nipple-cushions. Norks. Orbs. Peaches. Peaks. Pillows. Pilots. Pontoons. Rack. Stack. TaTas. Tater-sacks. Teats. Tits. Torpedoes. Udders. Upper-Frontal-Super-Structure. Winnebagos. Yahbos.

D

High school is a time of infamy. I am fifteen. I am a petulant and rebellious child vacationing in a woman's body. Businessmen stop to watch as I pass them on the street. Strangers sit close beside me at bus stops. Cars slow down and follow me as I walk home from school.

My overture is the swell of whispers and snickers in the hallway at lunch, my applause the straying hands in the crush of bodies on the stairs during class change. Though I feel miscast in the role of sex object, my body leaves me few options, so I play the part flawlessly. I read every book I can find on sexual performance and technique, every pamphlet on how to avoid pregnancy and disease.

I become an expert on birth control and STDs. I counsel other girls on which clinics to go to and what to expect.

High school offers no shortage of young men eager to explore the mountainous landscape under my shirt. I tell them I'm on the debate team. I tell them I've written a feature-length screenplay. They tell me I'd make a great stripper.

I do just enough to stay on the honour roll each term. I'm a good listener and don't need to study. I cut more often than I attend. I shave off half my hair, wear ripped clothes and black lipstick. Even with safety pins through my ears and an inch of smudged eyeliner, the right dress never fails to brighten a male teacher's eyes. "Where were you when I was in high school?"

DD

I am nineteen. I work as a switchboard operator at city hall. On casual Friday, I wear a pair of baggy jeans and a loose T-shirt with the "Guess" clothing logo across the front. Before lunch, one male employee asks if I want him to guess my bra size and another asks if he's supposed to guess whether "they" are real or not. An older female co-worker overhears this last comment and tells me, "You probably shouldn't wear that again."

I become more aware of how women react to my body. I have honed an edge, a hardness to deflect the onslaught of "Hey Baby"s. I've heard, always indirectly, that women find me cold and unfriendly. I try to make more female friends at city hall by wearing glasses instead of contacts, by not wearing makeup, by hiding my body under baggier clothes. But still, it is the men, not the women, who ask me to join them for lunch.

DDD

I am twenty years old sitting topless on a doctor's examination table. A man in his sixties stands across from me and stares intently at my breasts. "Quite a burden you've got there." He cups my right breast in his hand, holds its weight. His skin feels inanimate against my flesh. They must teach that in medical school. He doesn't make eye contact until his hand has left my body.

215

He asks me to fill out an insurance form. *In what ways does your body type impede your health and lifestyle:* I cannot walk down a flight of stairs without discomfort; I cannot jog, do aerobics or dance; no bathing suit fits me; I suffer from constant back and shoulder pain; I cannot stand up straight; I have permanent abrasions on my shoulders; I have to drive to Bellingham, Washington, to find bras in my size.

The doctor explains the surgical procedure using a black felt-tipped pen to draw incision lines on my body. We talk about results: given my skin colour, there will certainly be scarring. I should be able to breastfeed, though there are no guarantees.

Outside his office, his receptionist and I check our books and set a date as if we're planning to meet for lunch.

DD

After surgery, I try to lift my arm, but the muscles, heavy with chemical fatigue, resist. Around my torso, tension pulls, as if I am strapped to the bed. Flat on my back, I gaze up through a fish-eye lens. A nurse hovers and smiles. "Someone's awake." She checks my pulse. I grab for her hand, but my fingers only graze her wrist. I speak, but all that comes out is, "…hurts." She adjusts my bandages. "We'll get you some Demerol."

The Demerol travels from its syringe into a tube that snakes under my skin and for a while, I close my eyes.

The tension returns, burning this time. As a doctor unravels the bandages around my chest, I wait for the tightness in my torso to release. He finishes, but there is no relief. "Demerol," the doctor says to the nurse.

I feel nothing in my arms and legs, but the pressure inside of my chest makes me cry. The nurse brings another needle. "I can't give you any more after this. I'll have to get a doctor."

The fish-eye is full with three doctors and a nurse. I can tell by their expressions I have missed something in the conversation. "You're hemorrhaging. We're taking you back into surgery." I sob through a narcotic haze. The nurse strokes my hands and face. I am dying. I am dying.

216

One of the doctors returns and touches his hand lightly to areas of my chest, gestures I see but can't feel. "We're almost ready for you." He smiles then turns to the nurse. "Morphine."

The drug ignites under my skin, a long, slow sear that swells then recedes, and with it, all my awareness of pain. My tears stop. I am lighter than air. I feel my mouth smiling. I wonder if I have ever felt so happy in all my life. They wheel me into surgery, and I wave good-bye to no one in particular.

D

I am sitting in my hospital bed finishing the fruit cocktail that came with lunch. Three doctors arrive for rounds: one greying, one in his thirties, the third closest to my age. Earlier in the day, my mother had helped me change out of my hospital gown and into the cotton baby doll I slept in at home. With no opportunity to bathe, I sprayed myself with perfume. Now, with three men standing at the foot of my bed, I feel like a tart.

The older doctor asks me to lift my nightgown. He reviews my chart with the other two, and when they finally look up, their faces soften. My breasts are small and taut and high. Rather than approach, the older doctor points out the surgical cuts by extending his arm and gesturing with his pen. He explains that as the tissue relaxes, my breasts will become larger, more supple, that they will hang more naturally. I am mildly disappointed, having found the rigid alertness of my new breasts quite amusing.

"What size were you before?" the young doctor asks.

"Thirty-four triple D."

A thoughtful arch in his eyebrows looks almost like regret.

C

I stare at my body's reflection in the mirror of the ladies' change room at Eaton's. The woman in the mirror stands in profile, slim, perfectly proportioned and completely unfamiliar. I take a step to the side and watch my reflection suspiciously. I run my hands over the fitted satin cups of the 36C bra. I haven't worn this size since the sixth grade.

A friend's mother once told us that in her day, saleswomen would throw back the curtain of your dressing room and announce, "Let's take a look at you," exposing your half-naked form to all the other shoppers. I am almost wishing for that. Wishing for the courage to go streaking through the department store and out onto the street.

My saleswoman is chuckley and stout with a thick eastern-European accent. When I open the change room door a crack, she stops folding empty bra boxes and scurries toward me, tape measure floating like a boa around her neck. "Fits?"

She stands beside me, and I watch her in the mirror, running her fingers under straps and hooks. "Good. Good." She puts her hand on my back and smiles at my reflection. "Is perfect."

❦

I like to tell people the story of the chili sauce and birth control pills. I embellish. I use words like "radioactive" and "mega hormone." I include my mother's frantic call to the doctor and his lighthearted assurance that nothing bad could possibly come of the situation. The origin of my breasts becomes mythic. Like my scars.

Pale and tough, these hand-drawn seams run under then up the centre of each breast, around each nipple. Because of the second emergency surgery, the marks are heavier and more obvious than the surgeon or I had anticipated. Battle scars, adornment. I admire them in the bathroom mirror. In bed, before I go to sleep, my fingertips retrace the scalpel's path, the history of my body written in skin.

BREASTS

Kate Braid

Everyone I work with
has a flat chest.
No tell-tale bra lines, no straps,
nothing between them
and a plain white T-shirt
when the sweat sticks.

So today when I catch a glimpse of myself
in a newly-installed window,
reflection of a woman
with breasts
      two, not small, rather nice
      plainly female
I am shocked

I wonder if men ever forget
their penises.

Adapted from the poem "Breasts," previously published in *Rough Ground Revisited*, Halfmoon Bay, BC: Caitlin Press, 2015

Acknowledgements

I must thank my family, especially my husband, James Daniell, whose support enabled me to work on this anthology, and my mother, Candace Johnston, whose friendship and moral support (in front of changing room mirrors and otherwise) remains crucial to my happiness. Thank you to each bra fit consultant who has helped me buy the right size and to all the customers who ever trusted me with their own bra-shopping decisions. Thank you to Norma Holland, for her inspiring gentleness. Thank you to Lorna Crozier, Andrea Routley, and the many other friends who showed their early enthusiasm for the project and helped me push to make it a reality. Thank you to Vici Johnstone for her input and assistance during the editorial process, and to Rebecca Hendry and Kate Kennedy for their sharp eyes during copyediting. Finally, my sincerest thanks to everyone who submitted writing. I'm incredibly grateful to all the writers who trusted me with their stories and poems and who taught me all the very many things it means to have breasts — what it means to the writers themselves, and now also to me, and the readers of this book.

EDITOR

RUTH DANIELL is an award-winning writer originally from Prince George, BC, who currently lives and writes in Vancouver, where she teaches speech arts and writing at the Bolton Academy of Spoken Arts. She is also the founder and organizer of a literary reading series called Swoon, which focuses on discovering new and innovative work about love and desire. She holds a BA (Honours) in English literature and writing from the University of Victoria

and an MFA in creative writing from the University of British Columbia. Her poems and stories have appeared or are forthcoming in various journals across North America and elsewhere, including *Arc Poetry Magazine*, *Grain*, *Room Magazine*, *Qwerty*, *Canthius*, *The Antigonish Review*, and *CV2*.

PHOTO JAMES DANIELL

223

Contributors

Joelle Barron is a writer, mother, librarian and school secretary from northern Ontario. She earned her master's degree in Creative Writing from the University of British Columbia in 2014. Her work has been published in *Arc Poetry Magazine*, *The Malahat Review*, *The Dalhousie Review* and others.

Marilyn Belak runs with the Dawson Creek and Rolla BC arts crowd. She is an alumni of Sage Hill, Banff Centre Wired Writing, MK wilderness camp, and VMI. Her poems are in *The Malahat Review*, *TAR*, *Leaf Press Monday's Poem* and anthologies, *Unfurled* and her imprint Windward Press. Marilyn's poetry is her relationship with her natural and social environment.

Nicole Boyce is a Calgary-based writer and editor. Her writing has appeared or is forthcoming in *Joyland*, *McSweeney's Internet Tendency*, *The Awl*, *Big Truths* and more, and has been shortlisted for *The New Quarterly*'s Peter Hinchcliffe Fiction Award. She's an MFA student in UBC's Creative Writing Program, where she's working on a collection of personal essays about nostalgia.

Kate Braid has written, co-written and edited eleven books of non-fiction and prize-winning poetry. Her latest books are a memoir, *Journeywoman: Swinging a Hammer in a Man's World* and a book of poems, *Rough Ground Revisited*. She first became acutely aware of her breasts when she became a construction worker. She divides her time between Vancouver and Pender Island, BC, where she got her first job in construction. See www.katebraid.com.

Moni Brar is a writer, educator, avid reader and travel fiend. As an advocate for education, a student of cultural connection and a lover of the human condition, she has travelled the world and worked in nine countries, each of which has led her to reconsider the collective human narrative. Her recent short story appeared in the anthology *This Place A Stranger: Canadian Women Travelling Alone.*

Devin Casey is a photographer and multimedia artist living in Toronto, Canada. He's a social services residential/commercial building operator by day, and an environmental activist by night... Visit his website at www.devincaseyphotography.com.

Lorna Crozier's latest two books are *The Wrong Cat* and *The Wild in You*, a collaboration about the Great Bear Rainforest with the photographer Ian McAllister. An Officer of the Order of Canada, Crozier lives on Vancouver Island with writer Patrick Lane, two fine cats, two turtles and many fish.

Francine Cunningham is an Indigenous writer, artist and educator originally from Calgary, Alberta, but who currently resides in Vancouver, British Columbia. Francine is a graduate of the Master of Fine Arts program in Creative Writing from the University of British Columbia. You can find her work in *The Quilliad, Hamilton Arts and Letters, Echolocation Literary Magazine, The Puritan, Kimiwan'zine, nineteenquestion.ca* and *The Ubyssey.* For more information you can find her at www.francinecunningham.ca.

Emily Davidson is a writer from Saint John, New Brunswick, living in Vancouver, British Columbia. Her poetry has appeared in magazines including *Arc Poetry Magazine, Descant, The Fiddlehead, Poetry is Dead, Room,* and *subTerrain,* and was recently anthologized in *The Best Canadian Poetry 2015.* Her fiction has appeared in *Grain,* and was shortlisted for *The Malahat Review*'s 2013 Far Horizons Award for Short Fiction. She is at work on a novel.

Dina Del Bucchia is the author of *Coping with Emotions and Otters* (Talonbooks, 2013) and *Blind Items* (Insomniac Press, 2014). Dina and Daniel Zomparelli are the duo behind *Can't Lit,* a podcast on Canadian literature. *Rom Com* is their collaborative poetry book from Talonbooks (fall 2015).

Lynn Easton is a writer and columnist from Maple Ridge, British Columbia. She's currently working on a series of creative non-fiction essays after completing SFU's Writer's Studio in 2015.

Sierra Skye Gemma's non-fiction has won *The New Quarterly*'s Edna Staebler Personal Essay Contest, *Rhubarb*'s Taboo Literary Contest and the National Magazine Award for Best New Magazine Writer. Her work has been published in *The Globe and Mail*, the *Vancouver Sun*, *Plenitude*, the *Best Canadian Essays Anthology*, *SAD Mag* and elsewhere. Find her online at sierraskyegemma. com and on Twitter as @sierragemma.

Susan Glickman is the author of six volumes of poetry, most recently *The Smooth Yarrow* (2012), three novels for adults, most recently *Safe as Houses* (Cormorant, 2015), the "Lunch Bunch" trilogy of children's books and *The Picturesque & the Sublime: A Poetics of the Canadian Landscape* (1998). She works as a freelance editor and creative writing instructor in Toronto.

Catherine Graham's most recent collection, *Her Red Hair Rises with the Wings of Insects,* now in its second printing, was a finalist for the Raymond Souster Poetry Award and the CAA Poetry Award. Winner of the IFOA's Poetry *NOW* competition, she teaches creative writing at the University of Toronto School of Continuing Studies where she won an Excellence in Teaching Award. Her next collection will appear in 2017. www.catherinegraham.com

Sara Graefe is an award-winning playwright and screenwriter. Her creative non-fiction has appeared in various magazines and anthologies, including *Literary Mama*, *Walk Myself Home*, *Telling Truths: Storying Motherhood*, *Mothers and Sons* and *A Family By Any Other Name* (shortlisted for a 2015 LAMDA Literary Award). She lives in Vancouver with her wife and school-aged son, and teaches in the Creative Writing Program at the University of British Columbia.

Esther Griffin teaches creative writing and English literature at Georgian College in Barrie, Ontario. She is pursuing her MFA Degree in Creative Writing at UBC and works on the Poetry Editorial Board for *PRISM* international Literary Journal, Esther is the editor of *twenty20: A Canadian Poetry Anthology*, a chapbook series devoted to publishing and celebrating her students' work. Please visit her website: www.esthergriffin.ca.

Heidi Grogan worked at a Calgary agency supporting sexually exploited women for fifteen-plus years. There, she received universally relevant wisdom from women who know about loss and reconstructed lives, and their gift most certainly informs her writing. Heidi currently designs curricula for marginalized youth, and teaches courses designed to help low-income adults who have experienced homelessness and addiction challenges, adults whose barriers to learning are getting in the way of their development of skills and capacities that would see them flourish.

Jane Eaton Hamilton is the author of nine books of short fiction and poetry. Her novel *Weekend* is forthcoming in 2016. Her memoir *Mondays are Yellow, Sundays are Grey*, retitled *No More Hurt*, was a *Sunday Times* bestseller and included on the *Guardian's* Best Books of the Year list. Her books have been shortlisted for the MIND Book Award, the BC Book Prize, the VanCity Award, the Pat Lowther Award and the Ferro-Grumley Award. She is the two-time winner of Canada's CBC Literary Award for fiction (2003/2014). Her work is included in *The Journey Prize Anthology*, *Best Canadian Short Stories* and appears in publications such as *Salon*, *NY Times*, *Seventeen* magazine, *MS blog*, *Full Grown People*. She lives in Vancouver.

Rebecca Hendry's writing has appeared in the *Dalhousie Review*, *Wascana Review*, *Event*, *Windsor Review*, *Room of One's Own* and numerous other literary journals. Her first novel, *Grace River*, was published by Brindle and Glass in 2009. She lives in Gibsons, BC.

Valerie Hennell has a master's degree in creative writing from UBC where she launched a fifty-year career as writer, producer, broadcaster, artist manager and lyricist. Her recordings have garnered four Juno nominations, Parents' Choice, NAPPA Gold and Canadian Folk Music Awards. She lives on Protection Island in Nanaimo.

Taryn Hubbard's poetry, fiction, reviews and interviews have appeared in journals such as *Canadian Literature, Room Magazine, The Capilano Review, Canadian Woman Studies, filling Station, Rusty Toque, harlequin creature* and others. Her chapbook *RE:* was published in 2014 by dancing girl press. She lives in Surrey, BC, and blogs at tarynhubbard.com.

Sadie Johansen is a twenty-four-year-old woman living on the southern coast of BC. She is in training to be an office manager while saving to finish her degree in computer science. After suffering dysphoria from a young age she transitioned from male to female at the age of twenty-one.

Fiona Tinwei Lam has authored two poetry books and a children's book, and has a forthcoming collection of creative nonfiction. Her poetry and prose appear in over twenty-four anthologies. She co-edited the non-fiction anthology, *Double Lives: Writing and Motherhood*, and edited *The Bright Well: Contemporary Canadian Poetry about Facing Cancer*. Her video poems have been screened locally and internationally. She currently teaches at SFU Continuing Studies. www.fionalam.net.

Nancy Lee is the author of *The Age* and *Dead Girls*. An Assistant Professor in Creative Writing at the University of British Columbia, she has served as visiting Canadian Fellow at the University of East Anglia and Writer-in-Residence for Historic Joy Kogawa House, the city of Vincennes, France, and the city of Richmond.

Maggie Wojtarowicz is a traveller, food lover and appreciator of beauty. While working as an engineer, she realized that her love for written self-expression has been her life-long companion. In verse and prose, Maggie shares her challenges and life-affirming experiences to add diversity to the way we perceive the world. She now has several literary projects in the works.

Christina Myers worked as a community journalist in the metro Vancouver region for more than a decade, garnering several provincial and national journalism awards in that time. In 2015, she joined The Writers Studio at SFU as a student and then returned in 2016 as a mentor apprentice with the narrative non-fiction stream. She lives in North Surrey with her husband and children.

Annie Parker is a cancer awareness and genetic testing advocate from Toronto. She lost her mother and her sister to cancer and began advocating for research into genetic roots of some cancers. After battling her own breast cancer diagnosis, Annie Parker became one of the first women in Canada to be tested for the BRCA1 gene mutation. Annie has now survived cancer three times and continues her work to support other families affected by cancer.

Julia Park Tracey is the Poet Laureate of Alameda, California. Her poems and poetry reviews have been published most recently in *Sugared Water*, *Sweatpants & Coffee*, *East Bay Review* and *Postcard Poems*. She is the author of three novels, two women's history compilations and *Amaryllis*, a collection of poetry. Read more at www.juliaparktracey.com.

Miranda Pearson was born in Kent, England, and moved to Canada in 1991. Her poetry has been published widely in literary journals and anthologies, and her latest collection is titled *The Fire Extinguisher* (Oolichan Books, 2015). She is the author of three previous collections: *Prime*, *The Aviary* and *Harbour*. *The Aviary* won the Alfred G. Bailey prize in 2006 and *Harbour* was nominated for the Dorothy Livesay Prize in 2010. Miranda lives in Vancouver, where she teaches and edits poetry and works in community mental health.

Laura Ritland completed her BA in Creative Writing and English Literature at the University of British Columbia and is a recent graduate of the Masters in Creative Writing program at the University of Toronto. Her poems have appeared or are forthcoming in magazines across Canada including *Arc Poetry, CV2, The Malahat Review* and *Maisonneuve*. She is the recipient of the 2014 *Malahat Review's* Far Horizons Award for Poetry and is the former Editor-in-Chief of *echolocation magazine*.

Zuri H. Scrivens is a writer, knitwear designer and two-time breast cancer survivor, born and raised in Vancouver, British Columbia. Currently living in Langley, BC, with her husband and son, Zuri divides her time between selling handmade knitwear through Etsy and writing her first memoir, an exploration of a husband and wife's shared bond of post-traumatic stress disorder. Zuri's work has also appeared in *Emerge 15*.

Allison Jane Smith is a writer and consultant living in Ottawa, Ontario. Her writing has appeared in *The Rumpus, The Ottawa Citizen, Nowhere, Travelife Canada* and *Killing the Buddha*, among others. Read more of her work at www.allisonjanesmith.com.

Betsy Struthers is the author of nine books of poetry, three novels and a book of short fiction. Winner of the 2004 Lowther Award and past president of the League of Canadian Poets, she lives in Peterborough, Ontario. "Amazon," included in her latest work-in-progress, celebrates her sister, Catherine Porter, on the tenth anniversary of her surgery. Dance on!

Kelly S. Thompson is a former officer in the Canadian Armed Forces turned professional and creative writer. She has a degree in Professional Writing from York and a MFA in Creative Writing from the University of British Columbia. She is the winner of the 2013 Barbara Novak Award for Personal Essay and was shortlisted for *Room* magazine's 2013 and 2014 Creative Non Fiction Awards. She can be found at www.kellysthompson.com.

Emily Wight is a writer, science communicator and cookbook author from Vancouver, British Columbia. She spends her day parsing the language of neuroscience, and her nights writing recipes and non-fiction. She has a BFA in Creative Writing from UBC, and her work has appeared in *Room*, *SAD Mag*, *OCW*, *Vancouver Magazine* and online. Her first cookbook, *Well Fed, Flat Broke: Recipes for Modest Budgets and Messy Kitchens*, was published by Arsenal Pulp Press (April, 2015).

Janine Alyson Young's piece almost didn't make it into *Boobs* because she was preoccupied with the demands of breastfeeding her newest baby. Her debut short story collection *Hideout Hotel* was shortlisted for the Danuta Gleed Award. She holds an MFA from UBC and lives on the Sunshine Coast with her husband and kids.

Daniel Zomparelli is the Editor-in-Chief of *Poetry Is Dead magazine* and author of *Davie Street Translations* (Talonbooks, 2012). Daniel and Dina Del Bucchia are the duo behind *Can't Lit*, a podcast on Canadian literature. *Rom Com* is their collaborative poetry book from Talonbooks (fall 2015).